WORLD RELIGIONS
CONFUCIANISM
THIRD EDITION

WORLD RELIGIONS

WORLD RELIGIONS

CONFUCIANISM
THIRD EDITION

by
Dorothy and Thomas Hoobler
Series Editors: Joanne O'Brien and Martin Palmer

An imprint of Infobase Publishing

Confucianism, Third Edition

Copyright © 2009, 2004, 1993 by Infobase Publishing

Chelsea House
An imprint of Infobase Publishing
132 West 31st Street
New York NY 10001

Library of Congress Cataloging-in-Publication Data
Hoobler, Thomas.
 Confucianism / by Thomas and Dorothy Hoobler. – 3rd ed.
    p. cm. — (World religions)
 Includes bibliographical references and index.
 ISBN-13: 978-1-60413-107-9
 ISBN-10: 1-60413-107-1
 1. Confucianism—Juvenile literature. I. Hoobler, Dorothy. II. Title.

 BL1853.H66 2009
 299.5'12—dc22

                            2008029656

Chelsea House books are available at special discounts when purchased in bulk quantities for businesses, associations, institutions, or sales promotions. Please call our Special Sales Department in New York at (212) 967-8800 or (800) 322-8755.

You can find Chelsea House on the World Wide Web at http://www.chelseahouse.com

This book was produced for Chelsea House by Bender Richardson White, Uxbridge, U.K.
Project Editor: Lionel Bender
Text Editor: Ronne Randall
Designer: Ben White
Picture Researchers: Joanne O'Brien and Kim Richardson
Maps and symbols: Stefan Chabluk

Printed in China

CP BRW 10 9 8 7 6 5 4 3 2 1

This book is printed on acid-free paper.

All links and Web addresses were checked and verified to be correct at the time of publication. Because of the dynamic nature of the Web, some addresses and links may have changed since publication and may no longer be valid.

CONTENTS

PREFACE

Almost from the start of civilization, more than 10,000 years ago, religion has shaped human history. Today more than half the world's population practice a major religion or indigenous spiritual tradition. In many 21st-century societies, including the United States, religion still shapes people's lives and plays a key role in politics and culture. And in societies throughout the world increasing ethnic and cultural diversity has led to a variety of religions being practiced side by side. This makes it vital that we understand as much as we can about the world's religions.

The World Religions series, of which this book is a part, sets out to achieve this aim. It is written and designed to appeal to both students and general readers. The books offer clear, accessible overviews of the major religious traditions and institutions of our time. Each volume in the series describes where a particular religion is practiced, its origins and history, its central beliefs and important rituals, and its contributions to world civilization. Carefully chosen photographs complement the text, and sidebars, a map, fact file, glossary, bibliography, and index are included to help readers gain a more complete understanding of the subject at hand.

These books will help clarify what religion is all about and reveal both the similarities and differences in the great spiritual traditions practiced around the world today.

Area where Confucianism is a major influence

CHAPTER 1

INTRODUCTION: THE MODERN CONFUCIAN WORLD

Worldwide there are about 6 million people who today call themselves Confucians. The majority live in Asia, more particularly east Asia, because the birthplace of Confucianism was China. Still, in Europe, in North and South America, and on other continents there are small numbers of people who identify themselves as Confucians. Most are of Asian descent. However Confucianism has an influence far greater than the number of its active followers would indicate. For more than 2,000 years Confucianism was the dominant philosophical system of China. As a result, it infused all phases of Chinese life. It is reflected in China's poetry and history, its government and social life, and the ethics that shaped society. Because Chinese civilization spread to Vietnam, Korea, and Japan, elements of Confucianism can also be found in the cultures of those countries. Although few Japanese would call themselves Confucians, the values of Confucianism still exist in modern Japan. The same is true of Vietnam, North and South Korea, Hong Kong, Taiwan, and Singapore. Even the

A street scene in Suzhou, China. Confucian principles are still influential in the relationships between family members, citizens and government, and in the underlying principles that shape and maintain good relations within communities.

People's Republic of China, whose Communist government repudiated the nation's Confucian past, cannot escape its influence.

WHAT IS CONFUCIANISM?

Confucianism is a system of thought based on the teachings of Confucius, who lived from 551 to 479 B.C.E. If only one word were to be used to summarize the Chinese way of life for the last 2,000 years, that word would be *Confucian*. No other person has had as great an effect on the life and thought of China as Confucius. He is the most revered person in Chinese history and is accorded such titles as Sage of All Time and First Teacher. Though he is called Confucius throughout most of the world, that name is actually the Latinized form of his Chinese name, Kong Fuzi, or Master Kung.

WISDOM OF THE PAST

For himself Confucius claimed no great originality. Instead he looked to a past era that he saw as a golden age. He told a disciple, "I transmit but I do not create. I am sincerely fond of the ancient. I would compare myself to our Old Peng who was fond of talking about the good old days." Confucius served as a creative transmitter of the wisdom of the past. From his study of Chinese tradition, he gleaned the teachings that would influence China throughout time to the present.

ORDER AND HARMONY

Despite the fact that Confucius lived during the troubled times leading up to the Warring States Period (476–221 B.C.E.), a time of turmoil when feudal states were contending with each other for dominance, his philosophy emphasized the ideals of order and harmony. Central to Confucianism is the idea that people should live in harmony, both with each other and with

The Golden Rule

Confucius taught a moral code based on ethics, humanity, and love. One day a disciple asked Confucius, "Is there one word that should cover the whole duty of man?" To this question Confucius replied: "Fellow-feeling, perhaps, is that word. Do not do to others what you would not wish them to do to you." Thus, from very early times, this "golden rule" became an important part of Chinese thought.

No portraits of Confucius exist from his lifetime. However, this 19th-century Korean manuscript shows Confucius in the robes that he wore according to ancient tradition. A similar style of folded robes is still worn for Confucian rituals and ceremonies.

Five Virtues

Confucius taught his disciples to be gentlemen. In his philosophy a gentleman was a person who had developed the five virtues of courtesy, magnanimity, good faith, diligence, and kindness; and a man with those qualities should employ them in governing the state.

nature. To attain those goals Confucius advocated a system of interpersonal relationships and good government. The system had a hierarchy, with age favored over youth and the only equals were friends.

To Confucius government service was the highest calling of all, because good government would bring happiness to all people. "The gentleman first practices what he preaches and then preaches what he practices," he said. Furthermore Confucius believed that through education anyone could reach the high standard of a gentleman.

THE FAMILY UNIT

In China the basic unit of society was the family. The family served as an economic, social, and political unit, since family members participated as a group in those areas of life. The family was the natural environment for moral training and the bridge between the individual and society. Confucius taught that it was within the family that the individual fully achieved his or her human potential.

Confucius stressed the duties and obligations of each family member and believed that each should act according to his or her particular role. Of the five human relationships, according to Confucius three were within the family: father/son, husband/wife, and older brother/younger brother. (Note that Confucius viewed the family as a patriarchal institution. He did not include mother/daughter or older sister/younger sister in his basic human relationships.) The other two relationships were friend/friend and ruler/subject.

The strongest of those relationships was that of father and son. The son owed respect and obedience to his father to a much greater degree than was required in European civilization. As an adult the son was required to pay the utmost honor to his father, even after the father's death. Then the son was responsible for offering sacrifices to his father's spirit. Known as filial piety, this duty to father became deeply ingrained in Chinese civilization. In return the father was expected to provide for his family. Similarly, children were also expected to show filial respect to their mother. The strength of the parents' authority was demonstrated when they arranged marriages for their children—a decision in which the children themselves had no say.

Confucius stressed the hierarchical nature of human relationships. Of the five relationships, only one was between equals—that between friend and friend. Age was favored over youth; thus younger brothers were subservient to elder brothers.

POSITION OF WOMEN

A wife was subservient to a husband. In childhood a young girl was duty bound to obey her father. When she married she entered into the family of her husband. She was expected to obey and serve both her husband and his parents. It was only when her own

Relationships within the family unit were central to Confucian teachings. Respect for the elderly was part of this structure and is a Confucian value that still remains important in the cultures of east Asian nations.

Kinship

Francis L. K. Hsu, a Chinese-American scholar, wrote:

The Chinese way in kinship gave the individual a great sense of security and the wherewithal to deal with the problems he faced in the world. Women who were not beautiful did not need to frequent lonely-hearts clubs. Their marital destinies were assured by their parents. Men who just hoped to get through life with minimum effort did not have to seek their own identity and make a world of their own. If their parents were not poor, all they had to do was to take advantage of the shadow of their ancestors.

(In Francis L. K. Hsu, *The Challenge of the American Dream*.)

sons married that she would have power over someone else: her daughters-in-law.

RULER AND SUBJECT RELATIONSHIPS

The teachings of Confucius were directed particularly toward government. The last of the five relationships was that between ruler and subject. Just as the son owed loyalty and obedience to his father, so did the subject owe the same respect to the ruler. Indeed the state, the nation, was seen as an expanded family. The emperor was regarded as the "father and mother" of his people. He offered sacrifices to heaven for the good of the people, the land, and all creatures under heaven. Aptly, the emperor's official title was Son of Heaven. Centuries after his death in 479 B.C.E. Confucius's philosophy became the official doctrine of the Chinese government. One of the many duties an emperor had toward his people was that of carrying out the rites that had been codified by Confucius.

FOUNDATIONS OF EDUCATION

After Confucianism became a state religion in 136 B.C.E. it formed the basis of the Chinese education system for 2,000 years. Confucius had said: "Study as if you were never to master it, as if in fear of losing it." No people were ever given greater incentive to study, for the one way to attain power and influence was through government service. And it was through state-run examinations that a young man could win appointment to a government post. So important was this that any child who showed promise was set aside by the family for intensive teaching and training. Families even built special "scholar towers" where the student was locked in day after day, year after year. The family and village invested in the possibility of his success, for from that fortune flowed.

Over the years a system of examinations was developed that emphasized the student's knowledge of Confucian thought. There was no greater prize than to pass those examinations. Great scholars were honored as the superheroes of sports are revered in the United States. Not only the student but also his family and village shared in the honor. A successful candidate was allowed to raise a flagpole in his courtyard and display a banner describing his triumph. Even more important, wealth, honor and status followed, not just for the successful candidate but also for the family and village. The examinations were open to most males regardless of class, although the years of study required to pass them meant that most candidates came from the wealthier families. Still, China offered a career for the academically talented, which meant that the brightest individuals were in fact the officials of the government. These scholar-officials, or mandarins as they were known, commanded greater respect and prestige than any other group in China.

Confucianism was a force for unity and stability in China. Over China's long history its ruling dynasties rose and fell, but Confucianism remained the social and governmental ideal. Throughout the vast territory of the Chinese empire scholars studied the same books and shared a common legacy. Although Confucianism developed and changed, certain core ideals remained and became a stabilizing force for Chinese civilization.

THE THREE RELIGIONS

Throughout much of their history the Chinese have practiced and been influenced by Daoism and Buddhism as well as Confucianism—faiths that they often combine in different ways.

DAOISM

Other than Confucianism Daoism is the most important native philosophy of China. Its legendary founder was Laozi, who,

> **In Essence**
>
> *The Dao pours out everything into life*
> *It is a cornucopia that never runs dry*
> *It is the deep source of everything*
> *It is nothing and yet in everything*
>
> (In Man-Ho Kwok, Martin Palmer, and Jay Ramsay, *Tao Te Ching*.)

Carving of Laozi, Buddha, and Confucius tasting sake, a Japanese fermented drink. There is no evidence of a meeting between these three great religious figures but they are drawn together to show the inter-mingling of these traditions within China.

THE THREE TRADITIONS

Of the three faiths Confucianism has perhaps had the greatest influence on everyday life during the long span of Chinese civilization. Because it became the state philosophy its values became deeply rooted in the ruling class. The mandarin, or government scholar-official, had to learn Confucianism to pursue his career, no matter what other religious beliefs he practiced in private. Confucian learning was also diffused at a popular level by local government. Thus, although both Buddhism and Daoism were very popular and influential during certain periods of Chinese history, Confucianism remained the most important of the three.

according to tradition, was an older contemporary of Confucius. A well-known Chinese legend describes the two men meeting. In many ways the two beliefs complement each other, fulfilling the opposite sides of the Chinese character. In contrast to the official and public nature of Confucianism, Daoism stresses mysticism and the world of the spirit. Daoism appeals to the carefree side of life, the importance of unconventionality, and a desire for long life or even immortality. Daoism teaches that it is better to "go with the flow" of events than to be consumed by worldly ambition; most human effort was to no avail anyway.

Many a Chinese scholar was Confucian in his public career, but in private life or in retirement he might explore the truths of Daoism.

BUDDHISM

The other major religion of China is Buddhism. It came to China from India in the first century of the common era. China and India were very different in terms of their history and culture, yet Buddhism found fertile ground in China. Its teachings of mercy and salvation for all beings struck a responsive chord. By the time it became established Buddhism had taken on Chinese customs and beliefs and its character became distinctively Chinese. Over the years it would, in turn, influence Confucianism and Daoism.

IS CONFUCIANISM A RELIGION?

Some historians have claimed that Confucianism is not a religion at all. They characterize its system of ethics and values as a form of Chinese humanism. Confucius himself said little on strictly religious topics. On being asked about the spirits Confucius responded: "When still unable to do your duty to men, how can you do your duty to the spirits?" Some of the controversy over the nature of Confucianism is due to the fact that the Chinese view of religion is different from that of the West. The Confucian sees religion as a form of education.

This does not mean that Confucianism is completely unconcerned with the life of the spirit. Although Confucius believed that men should strive to direct their own destiny rather than allowing spirits to do so, he accepted many features of ancient Chinese religion. He advocated that when sacrificing to the spirits one should assume that "they were there." Confucius prayed to heaven and promoted the ancient Chinese religious rites. He accepted the Chinese cosmic order that regarded heaven as a force in the affairs of humans. In addition, he endorsed ancestor worship, another important part of Chinese religious belief. Further religious features were linked to Confucianism when it became the official doctrine of the state.

Confucianism in China thus had a unique aspect. It was both more than and less than a religion in the Western sense. On one hand Confucianism so deeply penetrated Chinese life in all its aspects that it became an integral part of being Chinese. On the other hand it lacked the formal structure and the personal, emotional, and spiritual intensity of other religious institutions.

Language

In the Chinese language one word, *jiao*, is used for the two words *religion* and *education*. To a Confucian, religion's main purpose is to instill moral values in the person.

SAGE TO ALL GENERATIONS

Over time temples devoted to Confucius arose throughout the country. Sacrifices were offered to statues of the sage or to tablets with his name inscribed on them, more a form of showing respect than adoration. It would not be correct to say that Confucius was worshipped as a divine being or a god. As part of the traditional Chinese veneration of ancestors, Confucius was honored as the ancestor of the teachings of Confucianism. He was revered for his role as Sage to All Generations, though at a popular level this often became outright worship.

Chinese students studying at Tsinghua University. Confucianism placed great emphasis on study and learning and these Confucian values still remain strong in China.

Yet Confucianism had other aspects very like those of a religion. In a real sense the emperor acted as the priest for the nation. As Son of Heaven, he performed rituals and rites directed to heaven for the good of the nation. So too the father in each home was the priest for his family. His role in the rites for the ancestors was essential. Moreover the Five Classics—five books of Confucian thought—although not necessarily considered divinely inspired, were consulted for their wisdom and studied with unequaled zeal and dedication.

CONFUCIAN VALUES

Because Confucianism was so tied to the imperial system, it lost its exclusive role in the 20th century. After the last emperor was overthrown, in 1911, China sought to modernize. The Son of

Heaven was gone but Confucianism was so ingrained in Chinese life that it could not be so easily discarded. Modern Chinese thinkers and political leaders wrestled with the problem of how to adapt Confucianism to a modern state. Mao Zedong, the leader of the Chinese Communists, identified Confucianism with the system he sought to stamp out. After the Communist victory in 1949 Mao sought to uproot Confucianism entirely. Today, mainland China again respects the values and ethics of Confucius.

Outside China, Chinese peoples and the civilizations influenced by China still revere Confucius in various ways. In modern Hong Kong, Taiwan, and Singapore, with their primarily Chinese populations, Confucius is held in high regard. And in Vietnam, Korea, and Japan Confucian ethics and ideals remain part of the cultural values.

CHAPTER 2

CONFUCIUS AND HIS TIME

According to legend Chengzai, the mother of Confucius, had a dream before her son was born. She saw five old men (representing the five planets that were known to the Chinese) leading a strange animal. It was covered with scales, like a dragon, and had a horn protruding from its head. This Chinese "unicorn" knelt before Chengzai and spat out a piece of jade inscribed with the prediction that her child would be "a king without a crown." Chengzai tied a ribbon around its horn. Later, when she felt herself ready to give birth, Chengzai went to a rock grotto (cave) by a mulberry tree. Chinese tradition says that two dragons stood guard and two female spirits sprayed the grotto with perfume. A spring then burst forth from the rock to wash the newborn. As Confucius was born heavenly music filled the air and a voice said, "Moved by your prayers, heaven has given you a holy child."

The story of this heaven-blessed birth was added to the biography of Confucius by devout followers long after his lifetime. Indeed, Confucius has at times been revered as a god. However his achievements need no mythical elaboration. He was truly

The city walls of Qufu, the birthplace of Confucius in Shandong Province. This is the site of the Temple of Confucius, the cemetery of Confucius and the Kong family mansion, the name of the family into which he was born. Qufu remains a popular site for visitors and is listed by U.N.E.S.C.O. as a World Heritage Site.

one of the greatest men in Chinese history, and his teachings were heeded by emperors and common people alike for over two thousand years. Yet the real Confucius was only a man who looked around and saw disorder and misery. He wanted to do something to bring order—which he called harmony—to society. Ironically, at the end of his life he thought of himself as a failure. However in the centuries since then he has become "a king without a crown."

THE PANORAMA OF CHINESE HISTORY

China's civilization was already old when Confucius was born about 2,500 years ago. The heart of Chinese civilization was the Yellow River basin. However the Yellow River is also known as China's Sorrow because its frequent floods destroy as well as nourish. According to Chinese legend a series of sage-kings, god-like rulers, learned to control the river with dikes and canals. The sage-kings also brought other tools of civilization to their people. One of the sage-kings, Huang Di, the Yellow Emperor, employed astronomers to study the heavens and develop a calendar. His wife was the first to learn how to weave silk from the cocoons of a worm that fed on mulberry leaves. Yao and Shun, two other sage-kings, were known for their wise rule and devotion to the people's welfare. The last of the sage-kings, Yu, founded China's first dynasty, or ruling family, the Xia, which ruled China from 2100 to 1600 B.C.E.

Up to this point China's history remains only a tradition, for archaeologists have found no physical evidence that points to the existence of a Xia dynasty. However, the dynasty that followed, the Shang (ca. 1700–1027 B.C.E.), really did exist. Today's archaeologists have found animal bones from this period, covered with the marks that are the earliest form of Chinese writing. Oracles, or prophets, foretold the future by placing bones in a fire and then examining them for cracks and other signs that could be interpreted. Archaeologists have also unearthed Shang dynasty bronze urns that are sophisticated works of art. The urns were used as vessels in solemn sacrifices to the gods, or spirits, in whom the ancient Chinese believed. The sheer numbers of such urns indicate that these sacrifices were widespread.

THE DYNASTIC PATTERN

The Shang dynasty was overthrown in the 11th century B.C.E. The new rulers established another dynasty, the Zhou dynasty. This set the pattern for Chinese history for the next 3,000 years, right down to the 20th century. Dynasties usually came to power through military might, and the early rulers were energetic and powerful. Over time, however—perhaps centuries, perhaps decades—the dynasty weakened. Rulers became corrupt and lost their ability to govern. Then a new family seized power, giving its name to the dynasty that followed. Though each new

Hu Kou Falls in the Yellow River. About 5,000 years ago the first Chinese farmers planted and tended their crops along the river's banks, and it is the inspiration for many myths and legends.

MAJOR CHINESE DYNASTIES

Xia (legendary) 2205 B.C.E.–1766 B.C.E.

Shang 1766 B.C.E.–1122 B.C.E.

Zhou 1122 B.C.E.–256 B.C.E.

Qin 221 B.C.E.–206 B.C.E.

Han 206 B.C.E.–220 C.E.

Sui 589–618

Tang 618–907

Song 960–1280

Yuan 1280–1368

Ming 1368–1644

Qing 1644–1911

dynasty used force to take power, its leaders sought to legitimize themselves by an appeal to heaven. Heaven was the very rough equivalent of the Judeo-Christian God, but heaven was not personalized as God is within the Judeo-Christian tradition. Nor was it a pantheon, or collection, of gods like those in the Greco-Roman or Hindu traditions.

THE EMPEROR

The reigning emperor, the Son of Heaven, carried out certain religious rites that ensured heaven's continued blessings on China and its people. The emperor's right to rule was called the Mandate of Heaven. Sometimes heaven could make known its displeasure with the ruler through natural disasters such as floods or earthquakes. Rebels who sought to overthrow the dynasty often pointed to such events as signs that the emperor had lost the Mandate of Heaven. If the rebels succeeded in defeating the emperor's forces, it signaled that the Mandate of Heaven had shifted to a new family.

THE TIME OF CONFUCIUS: DECLINE AND DISORDER

By the time Confucius was born, in 551 B.C.E., the Zhou dynasty was clearly in decline. The Zhou king controlled only a small area around his capital, Luoyang, where he performed the religious rites that brought the blessings of heaven on China. The rest of China was divided into a number of states, each ruled by a man with a title that can be translated as "lord." These states continually made war on each other to increase their territory. Yet no lord was bold enough to overthrow the king and begin a new dynasty. Any who might have attempted to do so would have faced the immediate opposition of the other states. Thus the balance of power secured the Zhou king's position—but his weakness made this a time of disorder and strife. The common people were continually bedeviled by armies marching across the land. Lu, the state where Confucius was born, was small and particularly unfortunate in its location between several larger and more powerful states. The history of Lu, the *Spring and Autumn Annals,* records that Lu was invaded 21 times between 722 and 481 B.C.E.

THE ARRIVAL OF THE SAGE

Confucius's father, Kong Shuliang He, was the governor of Tsu, a small city in Lu. According to legend, the Kong family was descended from the Shang emperors through a younger brother of one of the rulers, although this legend may have been created to give Confucius a royal lineage. Kong Shuliang He fathered nine daughters and a crippled son. As he aged he worried that he did not have a suitable male heir to honor him after his death.

THE UNICORN

The unicorn, known in Chinese as the Qilin, is the mythological creature that plays a role in the legendary tale of Confucius's birth and appears frequently in Chinese mythology. This fabled creature has the forehead of a wolf, from which a fleshy horn grows; the body of a horse; the legs of a deer; and the tail of an ox. Its colors are yellow, red, blue, white, and black, it drinks only water, and it never eats or steps on any living thing. In China, whenever a Qilin was sighted, the omen was good. It is said that the Qilin appeared when a just ruler was occupying the Throne of Heaven or when a great sage was about to be born. The animal symbolized a fair government, long life, and the birth of an illustrious person. It was also the creature that every member of Confucius's family down to the present day saw as he or she left the house. It was painted on the main doorway to remind the family members that while they were part of the greatest family in China, they were not the imperial family. For just as the Qilin bows down to the dragon, so the family of Confucius was reminded never to challenge the right of the imperial family to be the first family of the empire.

Each Chinese home contained a shrine to the family ancestors of many generations. The living head of the family regularly reported to the ancestors on the condition of the family and, to ensure the ancestors' blessing, made sacrifices to them. Only a male heir could perform those duties.

THE BIRTH OF CONFUCIUS

Thus Kong Shuliang He sought a new wife to bear him a male child. He appealed to the head of the Yen family, which had three unmarried daughters. Father Yen asked his daughters which of them wanted to be Kong's wife. Kong was already 70 years old, and the two eldest daughters remained silent. The youngest, 15-year-old Chengzai, spoke up: "Our father has commanded us. I will obey. Why ask questions?" Her response is strikingly Confucian in character, for respect for parents is a keystone of Confucianism. Chengzai, as was the custom, was presented to the ancestors of the Kong family; now she had become part of that family. However, she feared that her husband's age would prevent her from conceiving a child. She went to a temple on Mount Nikyu to pray. According to tradition the plants and trees on the hill dipped their leaves to honor her. After the visit, she became pregnant and, in due course, a son was born to her.

Much of Confucius's official biography was written down by Si-ma Qian, a Chinese historian who lived in the century preceding the common era—nearly four centuries after Confucius's death. Si-ma Qian was a careful historian who openly doubted the legend of Confucius's birth. Even so his biography of Confucius was necessarily influenced by hundreds of years of tradition and accretion.

A MORE RECENT INSIGHT

In attempting to discover the "real" Confucius most scholars today rely on the *Analects,* a collection of stories about the master that was written by Confucius's disciples shortly after his death in 479 B.C.E. In form the *Analects* resembles the Gospels of Christianity. It contains Confucius's discussions with his disciples—22

disciples are mentioned by name, although tradition holds that Confucius had 3,000 pupils. However, modern scholars have found stylistic differences in the text that indicate that some of the stories in the *Analects* were composed later in Chinese history. Nevertheless it is the closest thing that will ever be available to a true picture of the man and his teachings.

A temple at the entrance to the Cemetery of Confucuius which lies to the north of the town of Qufu. Over time the cemetery has undergone many extensions to accommodate more than 100,000 descendants of Confucius.

CONFUCIUS'S YOUTH AND EDUCATION

When Confucius was three years old his father died. As the widow of an official, his mother received a small plot of land to farm. Confucius helped bring food to the table by hunting and fishing—though the *Analects* notes that he did not use nets or traps and never shot his arrow at birds nesting in a tree. He learned to drive a horse-drawn chariot. He loved music, played a stringed instrument called the se, and frequently accompanied his playing with song. In his own words, "When I was young I was of humble condition; that is why I had to learn to do many things." From his earliest years Confucius had a passion for study. How he received an education, and who taught him, remains a mystery, although there were schools for boys of noble birth and Confucius may have attended one of those. Like other students of the time he learned from books made of strips of bamboo bound by cords.

INFLUENCE OF THE FIVE CLASSICS

Confucius later declared that music and poetry were two skills necessary for a complete education. He probably studied a collection of 300 poems called simply the *Shijing,* or *Book of Poetry.* Some of these ancient poems extol, or praise, the ritual and rites of the rulers; others are love songs and descriptions of everyday life; all were meant to be sung or chanted. The *Book of Poetry* became one of the Five Classics, all of which summarize the culture of China in Confucius's time. By tradition Confucius edited all of the Five Classics into their permanent form and may have written parts of some of them. Countless later generations of

THE FIVE CLASSICS

- The *Shijing,* or *Book of Poetry,* contains 300 poems to be chanted or sung.
- The *Shujing,* or *Book of History,* contains documents concerning the history of China from the time of the legendary emperors to Confucius's own day.
- The *Chun Qiu,* or *Spring and Autumn Annals,* contains the history of the state of Lu and covers the period from 722 B.C.E. to 481 B.C.E., two years before Confucius's death.
- The *Yi Jing,* or *Book of Changes,* is a divination (fortune-telling) manual containing a great deal of folk wisdom that is still interesting to modern readers.
- The *Liji,* or *Book of Rites,* consists of three separate ritual texts and concerns the Zhou dynasty's bureaucratic system and the proper forms for many ceremonies, not only those performed by the emperor but also those relating to ancestor worship, appeals to heaven, and government and household regulations and instructions.

Chinese students had to study these works because of their connection with Confucianism.

Whether or not Confucius really edited the Five Classics is not important. They are significant because they formed the basis for his own teaching. Confucius studied these works and others and is traditionally credited with writing commentaries on them. His deepest wish was to do something to alleviate, or lessen, the suffering and disorder in the world of his time. Confucius found the answers to his quest in his study of the past.

The emperors described in the *Book of History* were wise and just rulers. Their subjects followed their examples, thus producing an era of harmony. For example the *Book of History* describes the Emperor Yao (ca. 2300 B.C.E.): "He was reverent, intelligent, accomplished, and thoughtful—naturally and without effort. His courtesy was sincere . . . The influence of these qualities was felt to the four quarters of the empire. Thus the states were harmonized and the people transformed. There was universal harmony."

HARMONY AND SINCERITY

Two words, *harmony* and *sincere*, occur over and over again in Confucius's teaching. Harmony—a state of affairs in which society works well and all people are at peace with each other—was utterly absent from Confucius's world, an era when people felt that strength lay in power and conquest. Continual warfare between states drained the resources of the rulers, the dukes, who imposed heavy taxes on their subjects to support their military expeditions and their own lavish courts, and who gave no thought to the welfare of their subjects. Sincerity was equally lacking. The dukes made a show of their devotion to heaven and their ancestors, but their personal lives—dissolute, pleasure seeking, corrupt—clearly demonstrated that their respect for traditional values was merely superficial and performed for effect without carrying sincere intentions. Over and over dukes made treaties that contained solemn vows to ancestors and to heaven. As soon as it became politically advantageous to do so, however, they swiftly broke those treaties. Family ties among the dukes were as easily broken. Younger brothers plotted against elder brothers, sons against fathers.

In his early years Confucius was appointed to the post of tax collector. He supervised the collection of farmers' rice and grain, making sure that it was properly stored. Yet his post only made him more keenly aware of how much the people suffered under the existing system. He saw other officials take bribes; he saw families go hungry because taxes were paid with the food they had grown.

Monument in Qufu, the town where Confucius lived. The monument is topped by a sculpture of two round coins with a square center which was the classical shape of coins for more than 2,000 years from the third century B.C.E.. The round shape of the coin represents heaven and the square shape represents Earth.

CONFUCIUS BEGINS TO TEACH

What could one man, without wealth or military power, do to change this world of disorder? Confucius founded a school. He gathered around him young men of talent and ability and began to train them. His goal was to make them *chun tzu*, which can loosely be translated as "gentlemen." He believed that these students, his disciples, could in time change society by serving as officials in the government. Confucius gave his students practical teaching in the six arts—rituals, writing, music, archery, chariot driving, and mathematics. However his greater concern was to produce men of character who, by their example, would change society.

CORRECT BEHAVIOR

Remarkably for his time, Confucius allowed even those of humble birth into his circle of students. His only requirement was that a student demonstrate the proper spirit and ability. He felt that a man could become a *chun tzu* through education and by practicing five virtues. The first of these was *li*, "correct behavior." His models for *li* again came from the past. Confucius habitually wore an old-fashioned forked headdress and a long-sleeved gown similar to those worn centuries earlier when the Zhou dynasty was young. Confucius would not sit on a mat unless it was properly arranged, nor eat meat unless it was cut into precise squares. Those affectations caused some to ridicule him, but he felt that personal behavior was the first step toward changing society.

FIVE VIRTUES

The sage tried to exemplify the five virtues in his own life. The Confucius who appears in the *Analects* is a warm, generous per-

The Ideal of *Ren*

Confucius said that outward signs of correct behavior (*li*) were not enough. One must reflect sincerity and inner spirit. In addition to *li*, Confucius emphasized four other virtues, the most important of which was *ren*, roughly translated as "benevolence" or "humanity." Before Confucius's time, the term *ren* was used to mean a ruler's benevolence toward his subjects. In Confucius's philosophy, *ren* became an ideal for all people to follow. In addition Confucius prescribed the virtues of *yi*, "honesty" or "uprightness"; *zhi*, "knowledge" (in the sense of moral wisdom); and *xin*, "faithfulness" or "integrity." These five virtues became the basic ideals of Confucianism.

A sculpture of a Confucian scholar in the Cemetery of Confucius at Qufu. The descendants of Confucius have been buried here over a period of 2,000 years and by the late 18th century the perimeter wall reached more than 4.6 miles (7.5 kilometers).

son. He taught through discussion and example. When students argued with him, he frequently admitted that he was wrong, stating, "You think I know a great deal? I don't." Apparently he was not a powerful speaker and in fact distrusted those who sought to influence others by force of oratory, or speechmaking. This has been a tradition in Chinese history: The written word was far more important than the spoken word.

At the heart of Confucius's teaching is the idea that society works well (harmoniously) when each person understands his or her proper role and acts accordingly. Confucians called this the "rectification of names," which is actually a very simple idea. As Confucius said, "Let the ruler be a ruler and the subject a subject. Let the father be a father and the son a son." In this way there would be harmony.

Confucius taught that harmony begins in the basic unit of society, the family. Sons must show respect for their father. Younger brothers must respect older brothers. Wives must respect husbands. The father must guide through example. Then the family would be harmonious. The family was a microcosm of society itself. In the same way subjects must show respect for their ruler. However, the ruler too had his duty—to treat his subjects as a loving father would. By doing so he would ensure harmony. This was Confucius's prescription for the ills of his time.

A RULE OF JUSTICE

Confucius found his ideal ruler in the *Book of History*. That man was the duke of Zhou, the younger brother of the warrior who overthrew the Shangs and established the Zhou dynasty in China in 1045 B.C.E.

When the first Zhou emperor died he left an infant son as his heir. Yet in striking contrast to the rulers of Confucius's time, the duke of Zhou did not seize the throne for himself. He ruled in his nephew's stead until the boy reached adulthood. The duke of Zhou governed his people with justice and mercy. He took care to protect widows, orphans, and others who were weak and helpless. Among the activities the duke declared as crimes were failure to sacrifice properly to heaven and the failure to serve the people well. It was Confucius's greatest dream to find a duke in his own time who would rule as the duke of Zhou did. Confucius did not succeed. Some of his students did in fact gain appointments as officials. Through their influence Confucius was given a post at the court of the duke of Lu. However Confucius soon realized that the duke did not sincerely want his advice and counsel. By that time Confucius had gained a reputation as a wise man, and the duke used him merely as an adornment to his court.

CONFUCIUS'S WANDERINGS

Offended and discouraged, Confucius left his home state when he was around 50 years old. Accompanied by some of his faithful students, he spent much of the rest of his life traveling through

A statue of Confucius in traditional robes in the town of Qufu, the birthplace of Confucius and the residence of his ancestors during succeeding generations. Confucius is often shown as an aged man to emphasize his wisdom.

the neighboring states, looking for a ruler he could influence. Confucius wanted the power to put his ideas into practice, yet his unbending insistence on principle kept him from attaining that goal.

Confucius eventually found a great opportunity to gain influence. The state of Chin was in the midst of civil war. The duke of Chin was a puppet in the hands of a family that had seized power. Another family had raised a rebellion and invited Confucius to join them. Confucius was tempted, for he would have a chance to guide affairs if the rebellion was successful. One of his followers chastised him for wanting to join the rebellious family, pointing out that the legal duke backed the other side and Confucius taught that a ruler must be honored. Confucius replied, "There may be something in what you say. However is it not also said that there are some things so hard that no grinding will wear them down? Am I a bitter gourd fit only to hang up out of the way, not good enough to eat?" (The bitter gourd fruit is soft and edible when young but tough and unpleasantly bitter when ripe.) In the end he declined the offer. Clearly Confucius was frustrated at his failure to obtain a high post. On another occasion he said, "If there were someone who would employ me, in one year I would make progress; in three years I would succeed." Yet no offer ever seemed sincere enough, no ruler virtuous enough.

During his wanderings Confucius visited Luoyang, the capital of the Zhou dynasty. There, according to legend, he met the other great sage of China—Laozi, the founder of Daoism. Laozi was the archivist in the royal palace, the walls of which were decorated with scenes from Chinese history. Confucius pointed to pictures showing the wise and just duke of Zhou. "Here," Confucius said, "we see how the Zhous became great. As in a mirror, we read the reason for the present in the past."

THE IMPORTANCE OF SINCERITY

Once Confucius turned down an offer of a government position because he felt the ruler was not sincere. One of Confucius's students criticized his refusal. The student compared Confucius's ability to a precious jewel. "Should I keep such a jewel stored away in a case," the student asked, "or should I seek a good price and sell it?" Confucius replied, "Sell it, by all means. I, you see, am just waiting for the price." The price was, of course, a ruler who would sincerely seek his advice and act on it.

However Laozi told Confucius, "The bones of all those of whom you speak have crumbled into dust; only their words remain. When the wise man finds work to occupy him, he travels in a chariot; otherwise he walks . . . I have heard it said that a good merchant carefully conceals his goods and acts as if he had nothing, and that a perfect sage makes himself appear a fool. Put aside your arrogant manner and your . . . excessive ambitions. None of that is of any use to you."

An orchid in flower. Confucius died in 479 B.C.E., thinking himself a failure. He called himself the "hidden orchid," which blooms where no one can see it. Yet he had taught better than he knew. For three years after his death his students remained in mourning at his tomb—a tomb that is still visited 25 centuries later. Confucius's pupils then set out on the task he had given them: to change the world. They succeeded. No Chinese person has influenced the lives of more people than the man his pupils called Master Kong.

In the year 484 B.C.E. Confucius received an invitation to return home to Lu. One of his old students, Jan Chiu, had earned the gratitude of the ruler by helping Lu win a victory against a neighboring state. At Jan's urging the duke agreed to give Confucius the honors he deserved.

Though Confucius was 67 he was still vigorous, and at last he seemed on the verge of gaining a position of respect, if not power. However when Confucius came to the duke's court he was asked how to make people pay their taxes. As a former tax collector Confucius was expected to have some ideas. Instead Confucius said that the people were only following the example of their greedy rulers. He declared, "The virtue of the ruler is that of the wind; the virtue of the people is that of the grass. The grass bends in the direction of the wind." Naturally this response did not endear him to the court. He did not receive an official post and once more settled down to teach. However in Confucius's later years he suffered a series of tragedies. His only son, who had disappointed him by showing little ability, died. Confucius was also disappointed in the abilities and behavior of several of his favorite students. His most successful student, Jan Chiu, saddened Confucius by acting more like a venal aristocrat than a Confucian *chun tzu*. Confucius told his students, "He is no follower of mine."

Then Confucius fell ill. In a dream he saw himself facing the sacrifices that were made to the dead. When his students learned this they resolved to give him the honors he had never won. They dressed themselves as ministers of a great ruler and gathered around his bed. When Confucius opened his eyes he said, "By making this pretense of having ministers when I have none, whom do you think I am going to deceive? Shall I deceive heaven? Furthermore, is it not better that I should die in the hands of you, my friends, than in the hands of ministers?"

CHAPTER 3

THE DEVELOPMENT OF CONFUCIANISM

According to Chinese historians, after the death of Confucius his disciples "scattered and traveled about among the feudal lords. The greater among them became teachers [of rulers], or ministers; the lesser were friends of teachers of officials, or went into retirement and were no longer seen." The disciples of Confucius had to compete with other philosophers, for Confucianism was only one of many doctrines debated in China at that time. The intellectual ferment of this period gave it the name the Hundred Schools.

CRITICS OF CONFUCIANISM

One Confucian who repudiated Confucius's doctrine and formed his own school was Mozi (ca. 470–ca. 391 B.C.E.). He attacked the Confucians for their excessive devotion to things ceremonial. And it is true that while Confucius himself stressed that it was internal feeling that made the rites meaningful, some of his followers became obsessed with form and detail. Particularly

The throne of the emperor in the Imperial Palace of the Forbidden City in the center of Beijing. Built from 1406 to 1421 at the command of Zhu Di (Emperor Yongle), the fourth son of the founder of the Ming dynasty, the construction of the Forbidden City required a workforce of more than a million people. Until 1911, the Forbidden City remained the palace and administrative center of the emperors of China.

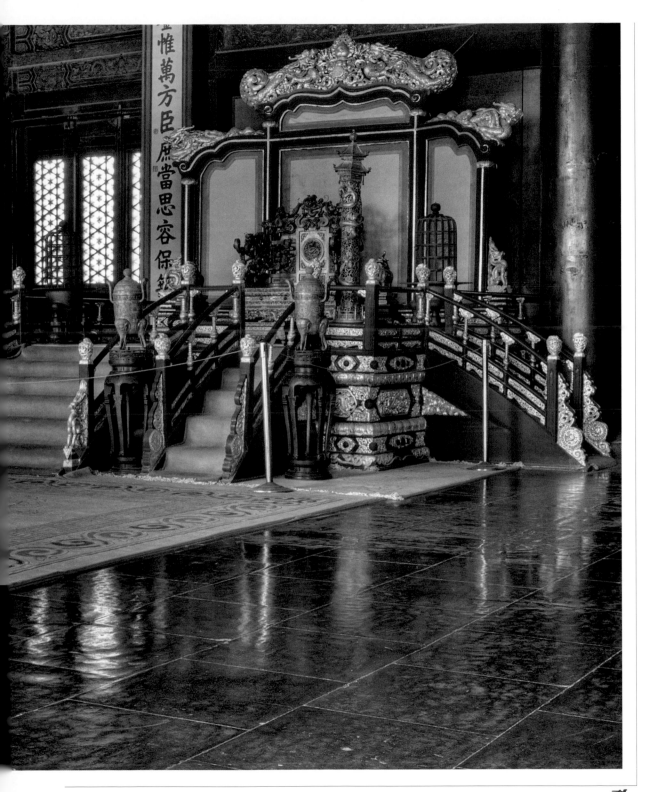

irritating to Mozi were the elaborate burial rituals and the fees that Confucians derived from them. He made fun of expensive funerals: "The funeral of even a common man would exhaust the resources of his family. At the death of a feudal lord the treasury of the state would be emptied to surround his body with gold, jade and pearls, and fill his grave with bundles of silk and carts and horses."

The basis of Mozi's philosophy was simplicity. People should seek only those things that could be proven useful for the good of society. People should clothe themselves adequately but not in various colors or fashions. They should eat plain food and live in simple houses. Mozi railed against music, which he believed held no usefulness and wasted people's energies. He also criticized Confucianism for its emphasis on family relations. Instead he advocated "universal love"—love for all people equally. Mozi had many followers during his lifetime and in the following generations, but his teachings were not destined to have a long-lasting effect on China.

Dreaming of a Butterfly

The Daoists would question whether or not people know what is real. The Daoist master Zhuangzi (369–286 B.C.E.), one of the great literary figures in Chinese history, wrote about dreaming of being a butterfly. When he woke he wondered whether he had really dreamed that he was a butterfly or whether he was a butterfly dreaming he was Zhuangzi. The Daoist affection for nature contributed to Chinese landscape art. It also provided a free-spirited alternative to official life.

LAOZI AND HARMONY WITH NATURE

Laozi, the founder of Daoism, although older in years, was Confucius's contemporary and reputedly the author of the *Daodejing,* the basic book of Daoism. He challenged the belief that knowledge and learning and a specific code of behavior would help people live in harmony. Laozi felt that people were naturally "good" and only needed to be left alone to stay that way.

Daoists shared with Confucius the desire for harmony, but their emphasis was different. Confucius stressed social harmony. The Daoists emphasized harmony with nature and its underlying "greater reality." The ideal of the Daoists was simplicity and a return to the state of nature. They felt that it was better to retire to a mountain top or to go fishing than be the ruler of an empire.

A COLLECTION OF PARADOXES

Daoist philosophy is the antithesis of Confucianism's concern for morality and the good of society. It stresses freedom of the individual, encouraging its followers to be true to your own character. Human beings are part of nature and nature is what it is—it can only be distorted by trying to impose standards of right and wrong. Daoism's advice can be summarized in a few words: *Relax and enjoy life!* However there is no point in striving to enjoy life, for striving is just another way of distorting one's nature. Daoism puts more stress on nonaction than on action. As one Daoist paradox says: The emptiness within a pot is what gives it its

The Chinese symbol for Dao above the entrance to a Daoist shrine. The Chinese characters that make up the word *Dao* represent the path or the way of the leader.

shape. It is best to accept whatever life has to offer. "Those who know do not speak; those who speak do not know," according to the *Daodejing*. The thoughts in Laozi's book are paradoxes that show the inadequacy of words at getting at ultimate reality.

Daoism developed into a popular religion based on the legendary feats of Daoist sages who flew through the air and were immortal. Popular Daoism offered potions for a long life or for immortality. Special diets and exercises were developed that promised miraculous cures. Since Confucianism was silent on any idea of an afterlife, Daoism's concern with these matters added to its appeal. Daoism would endure through the centuries.

CONFUCIANISM DEVELOPS

After Confucius the most important Confucian philosopher was Mencius (ca. 371–ca. 289 B.C.E.), the Latin form of the name Mengzi, or Master Meng. The two philosophers had parallel careers. Like Confucius, Mencius was a brilliant teacher and a disappointed government official. As a young man he had studied under a disciple of Confucius's grandson, and he always lamented that he had not studied with Confucius himself.

Yet there was a basic difference in personality between the two men. Mencius was immensely proud of his aristocratic background. His mother, widowed early, devoted her life to seeing that his education was a good one. When she died he mourned and buried her with such elaborate ceremony that his own disciples were embarrassed. Whereas Confucius often admitted to his students that he was wrong, Mencius was supremely confident in the truth of his teachings. Few were as skilled in intellectual debate as he was, and he made the most of it. He traveled with a large entourage and, through the force of his personality, intimidated several dukes into supporting him and his followers for as long they stayed in their domains.

SCHOLARS AND RULERS

Even more than Confucius himself, Mencius was optimistic about human nature. He believed that people were born good.

THE TEACHINGS OF MENCIUS

The teachings of Mencius contributed to the sharp division between physical and intellectual labor that became so entrenched in Chinese society in later centuries. The long fingernails cultivated by the mandarins, or imperial scholar-officials, showed that they never did physical work. Mencius described the scholar as follows:

> Dwelling in the wide house of the world, occupying his correct place in the world, walking in the great way of the world; when his desire for office is fulfilled, practicing his principles along with others; when that desire is disappointed, practicing them alone; riches and honors cannot corrupt him, poverty and mean conditions cannot change him, authority and power cannot make him bend the knee: such is the truly great man.

(In H.G. Creel, *Chinese Thought from Confucius to Mao Tse-tung.*)

Physical labor—a farmer harvesting rice in the traditional manner with a water buffalo in Guangxi Province, China.

The *Mencius*

Mencius's teachings are set down in a book called, simply, *Menzi,* or the *Mencius.* Mencius fervently defended Confucianism against the other schools of thought of the day. One such school was founded by Mozi, a Confucian who rejected Confucius's emphasis of family relations and advocated "universal love." Mencius attacked Mozi's followers for their doctrine of universal love. He believed that it was unrealistic not to put one's own family first. If one did not have special feelings for family, one could not love others.

As an example he pointed to the protective reaction that all people have to a child in danger. He urged his followers to seek "the lost child's mind" within themselves. In Mencius's view Confucian values were not externally acquired: "They are securely in us."

Mencius believed that it was every person's duty to reach his or her potential through study. More strongly than Confucius himself, he made the scholar his ideal. He boldly stated that the wise had a right to rule the physically strong.

Mencius shared with Confucius the belief that the ruler's role was essential to the good of the country. If his rule was inadequate, catastrophes both human and natural would result. Mencius emphasized the ruler's duty to ensure the welfare of the governed. When the ruler failed to meet his obligation he would lose his Mandate of Heaven, or right to rule. It would become the right or even the duty of his subjects to overthrow him.

XUNZI

Another Confucian thinker who lived after Mencius was Xunzi (fl. 289–238 B.C.E.). Xunzi was much more tough-minded than Mencius. In his universe nature and heaven were oblivious to humankind. Prayers had no effect. Whether the ruler was villainous or benevolent could not influence the course of the planets. The Confucian rituals were important not to ensure the good order of the world but as an outlet for such human emotions as joy and grief. Xunzi had a completely different view of the innate nature of humans. He believed that all people were born with a tendency to be greedy and bad. The saving grace was that humans could be trained to see the good and then follow it. Rewards and punishments would help miscreants see the light.

Xunzi's disciples developed the latter part of his thinking into the school of legalism. The legalists believed that the well-being of the state came before the individual. Acting as advisors of the state of Qin in the west of China, they encouraged the Qin king to wage war to increase the power of his state. The Qin ruler overthrew the Zhou king, leaving no Son of Heaven to perform the sacrifices. Then the Qin armies conquered the rest of the states and spread Qin rule farther south to today's northern Vietnam.

THE FIRST EMPEROR

In 221 B.C.E. the Qin king took the name Shi Huangdi, or First Emperor. Shi Huangdi's legalist advisors enforced his decrees and laws by prescribing a series of punishments and rewards. They ignored the tradition of China's past and declared that all actions must be done for the good of the state.

Confucians criticized those ideas. In the Confucian view the ruler should guide through his own example, not by laws and

Shi Huangdi, the First Emperor, controlled a far greater domain than any previous Chinese ruler. From the name of his state (Qin was formerly spelled Ch'in in English) comes our name for the country. His burial mound was surrounded by thousands of larger-than-life terracotta warriors that were discovered only in 1974.

punishments. Confucius felt that the ruler's actions must be done for the good of the people. Thus the legalists persuaded Shi Huangdi that the Confucians were his enemies. He responded in typical ruthless fashion. In 213 B.C.E. he ordered the burning of all books except those on practical matters such as agriculture and medicine. It is said that he also had more than 400 scholars buried alive. His reign was the low point for Confucians.

CONFUCIANISM BECOMES STATE DOCTRINE

Shi Huangdi's empire did not long outlast his death in 210 B.C.E. After a period of fighting, a commoner named Liu Bang seized power and formed the Han dynasty (206 B.C.E.–220 C.E.). Liu was a crude man who had little use for scholars. To show his contempt he once urinated into a scholar's hat. However Liu's advisers pointed out the uses that Confucianism could have in securing his power. Liu Bang's most immediate need was to stop his rowdy warriors from destroying his palace during their drinking bouts. Confucian scholars advised him to reestablish the ancient rituals to bring a sense of decorum and dignity to the court.

With Liu Bang's approval old copies of the Confucian Five Classics were retrieved from the places where they had been hidden during Shi Huangdi's book-burning frenzy. The Confucians' role as preservers and interpreters of the classics increased their power at the court. In 136 B.C.E. the Han emperor Wu Di proclaimed Confucianism the state religion of China. The dream of Confucius—to be an adviser to a great ruler—was fulfilled four centuries after his death.

THE EXAMINATION SYSTEM

The examination system had enormous influence in China. Because people throughout the country were studying the same Five Classics, there was a common culture throughout the vast empire. To pass the examinations became the goal of every ambitious young man. Some students took the exams over and over, trying futilely to pass even into their old age. Close bonds were formed among scholars who had passed the final examination at the Han Dynasty capital, Changan, in the same year.

CHINESE CIVIL SERVICE

A national university was established in Changan, the Han Dynasty capital, to train budding scholars in Confucian doctrine. The emperor tested the scholars on their knowledge of Confucian thought and some of them were picked for government jobs. Now the Confucian teachings could be used as the master had hoped—to guide the official in giving advice to the ruler. In this manner the Chinese examination system began. Two thousand years before the West established a civil service system, China had its own civil service system based on merit; the examinations established a candidate's qualifications. Over time the examination system would become virtually the only road to advancement in China.

THE FORCES OF YIN AND YANG

State Confucianism, the official form taught by Han scholars, was different from the original teachings of Confucius. Although

The yin-yang symbol surrounded by the hexagrams of the *Yi Jing*. The yin-yang symbol is a circle divided by a curving line into two sections, one dark (yin), one light (yang). A small portion of the opposite color appears in each section to show that yin always contains some yang and vice versa.

legalism was now discredited many of its ideas could be found in Han Confucianism, such as the absolute power of the emperor. In addition, state Confucianism incorporated early Chinese ideas on the cosmos that had not been important to Confucius himself. The Chinese believed that the universe was constantly influenced by two opposing forces: yin and yang. Yin is a creative force, associated with attributes such as dark, feminine, and cold. Yang is a dynamic force whose attributes include bright, masculine, and hot. The two forces are constantly changing in power, yet each is necessary for balance. The symbol of this belief is a circle with a curve in the shape of an elongated **S** dividing the two forces. Within each section is a small circular area containing the opposing force, thus demonstrating that there is always some yin in yang and vice versa.

THE FIVE ELEMENTS

Related to the yin and yang concept is the idea that all things are composed of the five elements—wood, metal, fire, water, and earth. Like yin and yang, these elements are continually influencing each other in the balance of nature. Wood is shaped by metal, metal is melted by fire, fire is extinguished by water, water is channeled by earth, earth is broken by wood, which is shaped by metal . . . and so on. The number 5 had great significance in the Chinese view of the universe. Each of the five elements was identified with five colors, the five directions (the center was considered a direction as well as north, south, east, and west), the five principal grains, the five planets (those that could be seen without using a telescope), and so on, through almost every field of human experience. Using this intellectual foundation, Han scholars analyzed and categorized the world of nature to produce a cosmogony, a study of the evolution of the universe, to determine how all things should work in harmony, the basic Confucian idea. Then they could prescribe ways of correcting imbalances, or disharmony. Their discoveries were used in medicine, nutrition, agriculture, art, and literature. Because of their link with universal harmony, these ideas became part of Confucianism.

THE FIVE ELEMENTS

The relationships among the Five Elements corresponded to many aspects of daily life and religious ceremony. Each of the elements had its "proper" counterpart in other categories. This chart shows some of the correspondences of the Five Elements.

THE FIVE ELEMENTS

ASPECT OF DAILY LIFE	WOOD	FIRE	EARTH	METAL	WATER
Seasons	spring	summer		autumn	winter
Animals	sheep	fowl	ox	dog	pig
Grains	wheat	beans	panicled millet	hemp	millet
Organs	spleen	lungs	heart	liver	kidneys
Numbers	eight	seven	five	nine	six
Colors	green	red	yellow	white	black
Tastes	sour	bitter	sweet	acrid	salty
Smells	goatish	burning	fragrant	rank	rotten
Directions	east	south	center	west	north
Creatures	scaly	feathered	naked	hairy	shell-covered
Beasts of the directions	Green Dragon	Scarlet Bird	Yellow Dragon	White Tiger	Black Tortoise
Virtues	benevolence	wisdom	faith	righteousness	decorum
Planets	Jupiter	Mars	Saturn	Venus	Mercury
Officers	Minister of Agriculture	Minister of War	Minister of Works	Minister of Interior	Minister of Justice

Details of a headstone in the cemetery belonging to the family of Confucius in Qufu, Shandong Province. Performing correct funeral rites and honoring the ancestors were central to Confucian conduct.

SACRIFICE TO CONFUCIUS

Confucius had always been revered by his followers. His descendants continued to offer sacrifices at his tomb in Li. In the Han period those sacrifices went beyond the ordinary ancestor worship that most Chinese families followed. The *Book of Rites* approved of public sacrifices honoring the great men of the past. Accordingly, now that Confucius's doctrine was the state religion, Han rulers made him the object of devotions that took on the trappings of a cult. Confucius was posthumously granted the title of Duke Ni, a title that passed to his descendants down to the 20th century. In 59 C.E. the emperor Mingdi ordered that Confucius be venerated in the schools. Scholars revered him as their patron. Mingdi himself made offerings at a temple that had been built at the ancestral home of Confucius. Over time the sacrifices of the state religion included rites to Confucius as well as to heaven, earth, many nature gods, and the imperial ancestors.

THE CHALLENGE OF BUDDHISM

During the middle of the first century of the common era Buddhism was brought into China from India. It came in the form known as the *Mahayana,* or "Greater Vehicle." Mahayana Buddhism offered a means to the liberation from suffering through the practice of compassion, as taught and exemplified by "bodhisattvas"—enlightened beings who would forego their own liberation until all other beings had been liberated. Buddhism provided strong metaphysics and a sublime art, as well as the appeal of transcending material existence.

Buddhism was completely different from any of the traditional Chinese philosophies. None had assumed the existence of any kind of afterlife. Buddhism, on the other hand, assumed an endless cycle of rebirth on the "Wheel of Life" and, if one followed the doctrine elaborated by its founder, the achievement of the state of Nirvana, or bliss.

Buddhism introduced speculations about the ultimate nature of cosmic reality, heavens and hells that challenged the imagination, ages beyond imagining. Confucianism had concentrated on the nature of experience and was silent on the nature of invisible powers. Buddhism had a sophisticated doctrine of *karma,* the effect of a person's deeds during his or her existence that would determine one's destiny in rebirth. Confucianism did not include the ability to gain rewards for a future life. Buddhism also had an order of monastic life that pledged its members to celibacy. It enabled women and younger sons to escape from the sometimes stifling Confucian family hierarchy.

A statue of the Reclining Buddha in the Jade Buddha Temple in Shanghai. When the Buddha is portrayed in this reclining position it represents *parinirvana,* the stage before the Buddha finally attains release from the cycles of death and rebirth.

Chinese Buddhism

As Buddhism became a part of Chinese life, Chinese varieties of it developed in its new home. Buddhism revered those who had attained the qualities of the Buddha and manifested the Buddha's perfection in various human forms. Chinese Buddhists "adopted" Confucius and Laozi as manifestations of the supreme virtue and wisdom of the Buddha. Moreover, the importance of the family was stressed in Chinese Buddhism.

THE APPEAL OF BUDDHISM

The arrival of Buddhism posed a challenge to Confucianism. Mahayana Buddhism's ideas of a "Pure Land"—a spiritual level of existence inhabited by a panoply of benevolent buddhas and bodhisattvas—had more popular appeal than the simple, rather strict Confucian ideals of harmony and virtue. Confucius had prescribed a system of ethics as a remedy for the disorder of his time. Han emperors, seeing the advantages Confucianism held for their rule, had adopted it. For the ordinary person, Confucianism provided a social framework and rites that honored the dead, but the founder of Buddhism had more directly addressed their sufferings. The Buddha's message offered the promise of transcendence and the reassurance that people could attain a form of salvation through the transformation of their own actions if they were motivated by compassion. This had strong appeal for the vast majority of Chinese, whose lives were filled with toil and who had nothing to look forward to but the solace of death.

After the fall of the Han dynasty in 220 C.E. China experienced more than 350 years of disunity. Buddhism spread rapidly. Without a central government the lure of government posts no longer impelled so many young men to study the Confucian Five Classics. Even Confucian scholars were influenced by Buddhism's highly developed view of the purpose of human existence. During this time a new form of Buddhism, called Chan, developed in China, which incorporated the practical Chinese view of the world. Chan Buddhists believed that everyone had the buddhahood within himself or herself. Through discipline and meditation each person had the capacity to achieve enlightenment while carrying on a regular way of life. This promised enlightenment, the goal of Buddhism, in this lifetime, without the need for endless rebirths.

DAOIST GROWTH

Daoism was also making inroads at the expense of Confucianism, taking on many aspects of Buddhism. There were Daoist orders of monks and nuns and Daoists had adopted many Buddhist forms of meditation. From the third to the sixth centuries, Buddhism was the dominant intellectual and spiritual influence in China, followed by Daoism. Therefore, when the Chinese empire was reunited at the end of the sixth century, Buddhism and Daoism were strongly entrenched.

During the Tang dynasty (618–907) China experienced a flowering of culture and philosophy. In the early days of the dynasty the model ruler Tai Zong set the tone for a vigorous policy that gave support to the three teachings of Buddhism, Daoism, and Confucianism. Tai Zong gathered a group of Confucian scholars at Changan to help him rule. He opened schools for the training of officials; the course of study included the Confucian Five Classics and commentaries on them. Officials trained in Confucianism headed the six ministries that controlled affairs of state. Personally the emperor favored Daoism, for he claimed descent from its founder, Laozi, himself. However, he also recognized the great influence that Buddhism had accumulated and so gave official patronage to its temples and monasteries.

The emperor saw Confucianism's importance to education and governance but felt that it ought to have a religious element. Thus in 630 he decreed that Confucian temples be established in every important town and city throughout his realm and government officials be required to make regular sacrifices in them. The temples contained tablets inscribed with the names of Confucius and Yen Hui, Confucius's favorite disciple. In 647 additional tablets were placed in the temples, listing the names of 22 famous Confucian scholars of earlier times. In the centuries that followed, the names of other scholars and distinguished officials were added to the list of those venerated in Confucian temples.

INTERMINGLING RELIGIOUS TRADITIONS

At some point statues of Confucius were erected in the temples, making them more like those of Buddhism and Daoism. The distinguishing features of the three faiths became blurred. More and more images and tablets appeared in the Confucian temples, imitating the colorful paintings and statues of bodhisattvas in Buddhist temples. Confucius was treated as a divine being, with special sacrifices made to his tablet or image in spring and autumn. The great Confucian temple in Changan was the scene of the most elaborate ceremonies. The three highest imperial officials sacrificed an ox, a pig, and a sheep; prayers modeled after the songs in the *Book of Poetry* were chanted; and ritual dances and music modeled after ancient forms were performed. These rituals continued until 1530, when after much debate, the court ruled against this form of religious Confucianism and ordered the images to be taken down. Nonetheless the temples remained, along with the tablets containing the names of Confucius and many of his disciples and followers. This is the customary form of the Confucian temples that exist in cities all over the world today—even in the Chinese communities of San Francisco and New York.

REASSERTING CONFUCIAN IDEALS

As government officials in the Tang dynasty the Confucians acquired considerable power, which they used to attack Buddhism and Daoism. In the ninth century a Confucian official named Han Yu issued a call to "make the Buddhists and Daoists human beings again and burn their books." Han Yu scorned the superstitious practices of the two religions and assailed Buddhism for its "barbaric origin." He attacked the popularity of Buddhism and Daoism as harmful to the empire. Their monasteries attracted young men and women, taking them away from tasks that would add to the material prosperity of the state, and they became wealthy through the contributions of the faithful. They controlled large holdings of valuable farmland but they did not pay taxes on their land or crops, naturally a source of concern.

Anti-Buddhist Campaigns

In the years 841 to 845 the government launched an anti-Buddhist campaign, seizing the monasteries' land and secularizing, or restoring to lay status, the monks and the nuns. According to one account 4,600 monasteries were seized, 40,000 Buddhist shrines were destroyed, and more than 260,000 monks and nuns were driven from their religious refuges. Buddhism in China was never to recover from the persecution, though it remains popular to this day throughout China.

NEO-CONFUCIANISM

During the last years of the Tang dynasty Confucian thinkers began to reexamine their tradition. A new vitality came into Confucian writing that would reach its apex during the Song dynasty (960–1279). By this time both Buddhism and Daoism had sunk deep roots, even within the traditionally Confucian scholar class, and both religions would influence the new thinking. This reexamination would develop into a philosophical system called the School of Li in China and Neo-Confucianism in the West.

THE SUPREME ULTIMATE

Neo-Confucianism did not come about all at once. There were many competing schools of thought, each of which accused the others of being "too Buddhist" or "too Daoist." Indeed, all did draw inspiration from the other two faiths, but they supported their philosophy with ideas from Confucian tradition. For example the Neo-Confucians adopted the Buddhist idea that the universe is endlessly changing. However, they used the philosophy of yin and yang and the *Yi Jing* to explain this process. From the *Yi Jing* came the Diagram of the Supreme Ultimate. Neo-Confucians used the concept of the Supreme Ultimate to explain the origin of things in the universe. It became the basis of all later Chinese ideas of cosmology, or the philosophy dealing with the nature of the universe. The Supreme Ultimate is not the same as the God of Western religions. It is real but it is a force that produces yin and yang, which together influence the universe. Thus the Supreme Ultimate differs from the Buddhist concept of the Void, which is the ultimate peace of those who achieve enlightenment, or salvation. Neo-Confucians also adopted the mystical diagrams of the *Yi Jing* to show the relationship between heaven and earth.

ZHU XI

The most important of the Neo-Confucians was Zhu Xi, who lived from 1130 to 1200. As a young man Zhu Xi studied Daoism and Buddhism but turned to Confucianism. He passed the government examinations at the unusually young age of 19. Though his learning and thought made him respected, his ideas were not fully accepted until after his death. Zhu Xi believed everything has its own *li*, or essence, and its own *chi*, which is its appearance or substance.

The basis of his philosophy was *li*, or "principle." Though the word is pronounced the same as the *li* in Confucius's original teaching, the characters in Chinese are different. The *li* of Confucius is the equivalent of "correct behavior" or

ZHU XI'S INTERPRETATION

Born in 1130, Zhu Xi's version of Confucianism brilliantly summarized the theories of philosophers of the earlier Song dynasty (960–1279). He wrote commentaries on the *Analects,* the *Mencius,* the *Great Learning,* and the *Doctrine of the Mean.* The latter two were probably written by people inspired by Mencius's teachings and were chapters in the Confucian classic *Book of Rites* before the school of Neo-Confucians raised them to a separate status. These four books formed the basis of Zhu Xi's ethical philosophy.

"ceremony"; Zhu Xi's *li* was something much deeper. Everything that exists, said Zhu Xi, has its own *li*, its essence. However it has an appearance, or substance, called *chi*. A leaf and a flower are different because their *chi* is governed by different *li*. Though *chi* can be changed or even destroyed, *li* remains constant.

Buddhists taught that people accumulated bad karma through evil deeds. To obtain salvation people had to rid themselves of this bad karma by the performance of good deeds or by meditation. Zhu Xi's equivalent of bad karma was *chi*, which could distort and obscure the essential *li*. Zhu Xi firmly advocated the

Zhu Xi conceived of a Great Li, or Supreme Ultimate, that he sometimes compared to the Dao of Daoism. The Supreme Ultimate was not God, but the essence behind all things. Places in China, such as the Black Dragon Lake Park in Lijiang, Yunnan Province, with the Jade Dragon snow mountain in the background—an area often referred to as Shangri-la—conjure up images of this essence.

Zhu Xi's philosophical investigations also had a more practical aspect. He called for rigorous study of the Five Classics and the objective world in which people lived. Through investigation one could understand the essential *li* and learn how to act correctly. And this applied not only to the individual but to the state. Indeed, Zhu Xi often quoted his favorite text, the *Great Learning,* which describes the process as follows:

The extension of knowledge consists in the investigation of things. When things are investigated knowledge is extended; when knowledge is extended the will becomes sincere; when the will is sincere the mind is rectified; when the mind is rectified personal life is cultivated; when personal life is cultivated the family will be regulated; when the family is regulated the state will be in order; and when the state is in order there will be peace in the world.

(In Conrad Totman, *Japan Before Perry*.)

extension of knowledge, or the investigation of things, to rid oneself of *chi*. Zhu Xi likened "the investigation of things" to "dusting off one's mind," an idea that was similar to Mencius's concept of restoring the "lost child's mind."

Through this investigation, people could reach the fulfillment of becoming a sage like Confucius himself. Becoming a sage meant realizing one's essential identity and resisting the selfish desires and other unworthy impulses that are caused by *chi*. The sage does not become immortal, however. When he dies, his reward is peace and rest. This is comparable to the Buddhist goal of becoming a buddha through enlightenment. Indeed Zhu Xi sounds very Buddhist when he says, "If one could but realize that it is human desire that thus obscures his true nature, he would be enlightened." We can also see the origins of this idea in the teachings of Mencius, who said that people were essentially good.

Zhu Xi sought to bring Confucianism to a popular level by writing a manual for ritual and behavior that could be used by ordinary people. It became as influential as any Confucian work ever written and in later centuries was found in homes throughout China. Zhu Xi had an influence almost equal to that of Confucius himself. The commentaries he wrote on the Five Classics became the orthodox ones. For the next eight centuries candidates for the Chinese examinations had to memorize Confucianism as interpreted by Zhu Xi. Though the Chinese did not call the philosophy Neo-Confucianism, it was different enough to merit a new name.

WANG YANG-MING

A Confucian thinker who challenged the teachings of Zhu Xi was Wang Yang-ming (1472–1529), who lived during the Ming dynasty. Wang had studied both Buddhism and Daoism and found insight at the age of 36. It came suddenly to him, just as enlightenment is supposed to come according to the philosophy of Chan Buddhism. Indeed, Wang's philosophy drew heavily on Chan Buddhist ideas. He believed that intuition was more important than study and investigation in determining the truth. Each person had far more knowledge than he or she realized; looking within brought forth essential goodness and wisdom.

Furthermore, Wang Yang-ming said knowing the truth was not enough; it was necessary to act on it. This echoed Confucius's original teaching that following proper form was not sufficient—form had to be sincerely felt and shown in every action. Wang sought to make Confucianism a practical philosophy in everyday life by emphasizing the link of thought with action.

Though he accepted some Buddhist and Daoist ideas, he found Confucianism superior. He condemned Buddhists for running away from the world's problems instead of trying to solve them. Wang was influential among other thinkers of the time. As a teacher he had many followers. However his influence never overturned the new orthodoxy of Zhu Xi's school. His ideas, however, became important outside China, particularly in Japan.

INVESTIGATION OF A BAMBOO

Wang Yang-ming openly made fun of Zhu Xi's call for the investigation of things. He wrote:

Everyone says that in investigating things one should use the method of Zhu Xi, but how can it actually be done? I have tried to do it. Formerly I discussed this with my friend Chien . . . I pointed to a bamboo in front of the pavilion and told him to investigate it. Day and night Chien meticulously investigated the principle of the bamboo. For three days he exhausted his mind, until his mental energy was overtaxed and he became ill . . . I took up the task myself and investigated the bamboo early and late, but still I could not discover its principle. After seven days I too became ill because of having worn out my mind. So we sighed together and said, "The reason we cannot be sages or worthy men is that we lack the great strength that is needed for the investigation of things."

(In H. G. Creel, *Chinese Thought from Confucius to Mao Tse-tung.*)

CHAPTER 4

THE INFLUENCE OF CONFUCIANISM SPREADS

Confucianism sank deep roots, not only in the national belief system of China but also in the culture of such east Asian countries as Vietnam, Korea, and Japan. This was a remarkable phenomenon, for unlike Buddhism, Confucianism had no missionaries, monks, or pilgrims. The symbols of Confucianism in action were the official and the scholar, and they rarely left China. Moreover, the particular concerns of Confucianism were the family and the state.

Confucianism spread to other east Asian countries accompanied by the inestimable boon of Chinese civilization. The Chinese believed that their culture and learning were universal—open to all who would become civilized, not to Chinese people alone. The attraction of this culture was undeniable; it offered a writing system, sophisticated philosophy and religion, and arts of the finest quality.

Confucian priests during a temple ritual in South Korea. Confucian values had a wide appeal in east Asian countries, offering a system of governance, philosophy, and religion and a high standard of cultural arts.

A courtyard in a Confucian shrine in Nagasaki, Japan. Confucianism was gradually brought into Japan with visitors from China and Korea and it was under the reign of Prince Shotoku Taishi (576–622) that steps were taken to incorporate these new ideas, particularly in relation to government and education.

SON OF HEAVEN

In the Confucian order proper attention had to be paid to hierarchy. At the top of the hierarchy was China. Its emperor, the Son of Heaven, mediated between heaven and civilized people, or those who shared their civilization. (Those peoples who did not share their civilization they called barbarians.) In China's dealings with other peoples there was no question of equality. Other countries offered tribute. In return they were given presents (making this exchange a disguised form of trade). The Chinese emperor invested the rulers of neighboring countries with their right to rule. In practice the Chinese rarely interfered with the way in which rulers conducted their own government affairs.

China's neighbors eagerly embraced this culture. Educated people in Vietnam, Korea, and Japan could read and write, if not speak, Chinese. Communications on trade and diplomacy were in the Chinese language. The intelligentsia, or intellectuals who formed an elite, and the officials read the same Five Classics that were read in China, adding to the vast literature of commentaries on Confucian learning. Over time Vietnam, Korea, and Japan became imbued with the same Confucian values that shaped China. Their relationship with China was likened to the elder brother/younger brother model of Confucius's five human relationships.

THE MIDDLE KINGDOM

The Chinese called their country the Middle Kingdom and saw themselves as the center of the world. China had developed in spite of its isolation from the other great civilizations, and the early Chinese saw no people around their borders who had created any culture as great as their own. Those peoples who did not share their civilization they called barbarians. For centuries the Chinese believed that their civilization was alone in the world. Their attitudes framed their relationships with countries around them in what became the Confucian world order. The Confucian world order contained the same values as Confucianism itself. It was based on the understanding that heaven was rational and that the world should be ordered in a moral way to bring about order and harmony. These goals could be achieved by observing proper forms and rituals. This idea corresponded to the Confucian belief that performing actions correctly worked on the inner morality of humankind as well.

VIETNAM

The ancient origins of the Vietnamese are enmeshed in myth and legend. Living in the region of today's southern China and northern Vietnam, the Vietnamese became part of the Chinese empire in 111 B.C.E., during the Han dynasty (206 C.E.–220 B.C.E.). Under the control of the Chinese for the next 1,000 years, the Vietnamese absorbed much of China's civilization—written language, forms of Buddhism, methods of government and social organization, and Confucian ideals. The written Chinese language was used for administration and education. In the first years of the common era the Chinese governor of Vietnam opened schools to teach the Chinese tradition, which included Confucian ethics.

VIETNAMESE NATIONALISM

Even with a strong Confucian presence the Vietnamese clung to their own identity. They kept their own spoken language. Personal habits and grooming—long hair, tattoos, black-lacquered teeth, and the chewing of betel nuts (intoxicating seeds from betel palm trees)—were different from Chinese custom. Although the Vietnamese family was patriarchal, women enjoyed more freedom than their counterparts in China, or indeed in the Europe of the time. Both sisters and brothers could inherit the land of their parents. If a family had no sons, the daughters performed the ancestral rituals.

The Chinese occupation of Vietnam instilled in the Vietnamese a fierce sense of nationalism. In 39 C.E. the Trung sisters led the first serious Vietnamese attempt at

An incense burner and joss sticks in the courtyard of a Daoist temple in Vietnam. For a thousand years from 111 B.C.E. the Vietnamese absorbed many elements of Chinese civilization as they were part of the Chinese empire. Modern-day religious traditions in Vietnam often combine Daoist, Confucian, and indigenous beliefs.

independence. Their successful rebellion established a kingdom that lasted only three years before the Chinese regained control. Other revolutions also ended in failure. In 938, however, at the battle of Bach Dang, the Vietnamese expelled the Chinese and ushered in a new era of independence. Over the next 500 years, Vietnam remained independent and was ruled by six different dynasties.

RELATIONSHIPS WITH CHINA

The Vietnamese developed a new relationship with China, that of younger brother. The Vietnamese emperor paid tribute to the Chinese Son of Heaven and was in turn given a seal to show his right to rule at home. Although the Vietnamese ruler called himself king when he wrote to the Chinese emperor, at home he gave himself the title of emperor. He was the Son of Heaven in the Vietnamese universe. The Vietnamese emperor adopted the ceremonies and rites of the Chinese Son of Heaven. Tattoos were banned, first on the body of the emperor and then among his soldiers. As in China, because Confucian knowledge was the route to a government career, Confucianism steadily gained adherents. Court officials discussed the concept of righteousness and the proper way to show concern for public order.

The Vietnamese government developed a Confucian-trained civil service. In 1070 a temple of Confucius was built in Hanoi, the capital. Five years later the first civil service examinations were held there. These exams, held every three years for the next 844 years, required years of study and a thorough absorption of Chinese culture. Chinese language, writing, literature, and philosophy became a necessary part of the education of all upper-class Vietnamese.

Just as in China, thousands of students crowded the regional test centers to take the examinations, sheltering in tents pitched in large fields. Roll call was held the night before the test to ensure that only eligible candidates would take part. The tests started at dawn, monitored by mandarins who sat in watchtowers to spot cheating. (During the Vietnam War of the 20th century some of those test sites were used as airfields.) Few passed the rigorous tests, but even those who failed could become "village scholars" and serve as an important link between the traditional Vietnamese village and the government.

The Vietnamese scholars consciously sought to imitate their counterparts in China in personal behavior and in government administration. However, the Vietnamese chose models from periods in Chinese history—the Han, the Tang, and the Ming dynasties—as well as from the time of Confucius himself. For example, these are the words of a 15th-century Vietnamese emperor expressing his pride in Chinese culture:

The Quiet South (Vietnam) boasts polished ways.
Our kings and subject heed Han laws.
Our caps and gowns obey Tang rules.

Thus Vietnamese Confucianism developed forms that seemed particularly authoritative and appealing to Vietnamese.

"FATHERS OF THE PEOPLE"

From time to time the Vietnamese scholars launched campaigns to enforce Confucian orthodoxy (as they interpreted it) among the people. They encouraged the five human relationships, demanded that new Confucian temples be built, and even called for the adoption of Chinese dress and manners. Confucian values were reinforced by state decree. Vietnam's first comprehensive code of laws proclaimed that the family was the basis of Vietnamese society. Protecting the family was one of the goals of the Vietnamese state. The scholar-officials were known as the fathers of the people, and they served the emperor

THE "CHINESE LION"

The Vietnamese rulers built a capital city with a palace that was virtually an exact replica of China's Forbidden City—the emperor's residence in Beijing. The Vietnamese also imitated the Chinese in their dealings with their neighbors. At one point the Chinese emperor sent the Vietnamese a golden seal embossed with a camel to show that the Vietnamese "king" ruled with the emperor's approval. Later, when the Vietnamese extended their influence over the Khmer peoples (who live in today's Cambodia), the Vietnamese ruler sent a duplicate of this seal to the Khmer king. The Khmers had never seen a camel, and they called the beast on the seal a "Chinese lion."

as sons served a father. Over time the Vietnamese father wielded power over his wife and children, similar to that of a Chinese father. Legally he could treat them however he wished, though in practice the Vietnamese wife retained much of her traditional authority.

KOREA

According to Korean legend the first ruler and guiding spirit of the country was Tangun, who founded his kingdom, Old Choson, in 2333 B.C.E. Its capital was at Asadal near Pyongyang in today's North Korea. The earliest Korean religion was a form of shamanism (the belief in an unseen world of gods, demons, and spirits responsive only to the shamans, or priests) in which the spirits of nature were worshipped. A female medium, or *mudang*, made contact with the spirits by means of secret magical rites and charms.

Confucianism was introduced from China in the first century B.C.E. When Buddhism arrived about four centuries later the two religions competed for popularity. Throughout Korean history both have remained important. Koreans refer to shamanism, Buddhism, and Confucianism as "the legs of the three-legged stool," all part of the country's cultural heritage.

FLOWER KNIGHTS OF SILLA

After Tangun Korea was divided into three kingdoms, though all shared a common heritage. In Silla, one of those kingdoms, young aristocrats belonged to a military society called the Flower Knights. The knights regularly visited famous mountains, which were said to be home to spirits, and took part in elaborate ritual songs and dances to pray for the welfare of the nation—practices that illustrate Confucian influence. A Buddhist monk wrote a system of five rules for the Flower Knights: to serve the king with loyalty; to serve one's parents with filial piety; to be faithful to friends; not to retreat in battle; and not to kill without reason. These rules neatly combined both Buddhist and Confucian values and virtues.

When Silla conquered the two other kingdoms and united Korea in 668 C.E., Buddhism became the state religion. However, scholars traveled to China to observe the workings of the Confucian form of government. They returned with many Confucian texts and, as a result, Confucianism would provide the philosophical and structural basis of the Korean state.

THE YI DYNASTY

Confucianism triumphed in Korea with the founding of the Yi dynasty (1392–1910). At his coronation Yi Song-gye, the dynasty's founder, issued a decree proclaiming that the Mandate of Heaven had settled on the house of Yi. Song-gye called for officials to help run the kingdom according to heaven's will and promised the people that he would work for their benefit. Song-gye transferred the capital to Hanyang (today's Seoul, the capital of South Korea on the River Han) and began to make it worthy of a great dynasty. He established Confucian shrines to his ancestors and constructed palaces and government buildings.

The aim of Song-gye and the early Yi rulers was nothing less than to establish a new Confucian moral order. In the year of its establishment, the Yi dynasty made Confucianism the state religion. The form they adopted was the Neo-Confucianism of Zhu Xi, which had spread to Korea during the Song dynasty (960–1279) in China. The government set out to imbue the populace with Neo-Confucian ideals and to gain a pool of talent for government service. A public school system was promoted to teach Confucian studies throughout the country. The best scholars were honored at the temple of Confucius in the capital, and the emperor carried out the rituals honoring the sage in spring and autumn.

Later the Korean aristocratic tradition reasserted itself. A small number of aristocrats, or *yangban*, monopolized the government posts, which became restricted

Land of the Morning Calm

Yi Song-gye, founder of the Yi dynasty (1392–1910), renamed Korea Choson after the first ruler and guiding spirit of Korea, Tangun's legendary ancient kingdom. The name means "morning calm," and Koreans still call their country the Land of the Morning Calm.

MORAL RULE IN KOREA

The kings of the Yi dynasty (1392–1910) were indoctrinated in Neo-Confucian doctrine. The Korean scholar Yi Yulgok expressed the idea of moral rule in Neo-Confucian terms:

The study of the Way is to make goodness clear through the investigation (of things) and the extension (of knowledge) and to cultivate one's self through sincerity (of thought) and rectification (of mind). When (they are) contained in one's person, (they) become the virtue of Heaven and when (they are) carried out in government (they) become the Kingly Way.

(In JaHyun Kim Haboush, *A Heritage of Kings.*)

A Confucian scholar in traditional dress painted by the artist Yi Che-gwan during the period 1760–1840.

to them alone. The private academies that began to flourish throughout Korea drove out the public school system.

KOREAN FAMILY STRUCTURE

The spread of Confucian ritual and customs brought changes to Korean society. The Korean family had traditionally been different from that of China. Formerly a Korean husband went to live in the territory of his wife; women had equal rights of inheritance with men. However these practices did not conform to Confucian custom and the requirement that sacrifices be offered in the father's home. Under the Yi Dynasty the five human relationships, which gave greater authority to males, were enforced by the state. Over time Korean customs changed. Now the father's line became the more important and women lost the right of equal inheritance. In the past Korean rituals for coming of age, marriage, and death had all followed Buddhist forms. Now they were held in accordance with Confucian precepts. Zhu Xi's Neo-Confucian idea that the Confucian social order reflected the order of the universe was interpreted to mean that an attempt to change one's social status was a sin against heaven.

Approach to the main gateway of a Confucian temple in Gumi, South Korea. Confucianism arrived in Korea in the first century B.C.E. and four centuries later Confucianism was equally as popular as Buddhism. Confucianism is now regarded as one of the foundations of the country's religious heritage, along with shamanism and Buddhism.

YANGBAN TRADITION

Neo-Confucianism in Korea was observed more strictly by the *yangban* class than by the common people. Koreans had a saying: "Legal punishments do not apply to *yangban,* and proper behavior does not apply to commoners." The *yangbans* belonged to aristocratic clans that had played an important role in Korea from ancient times. Under the stimulus of Confucianism the *yangbans* traced their clan lineage back many generations. They established family shrines where rites to the ancestors were performed with pomp and ceremony.

The *yangbans* also took up the Chinese practice of arranged marriages. Marriage within a clan was forbidden, and so *yangban* marriages were arranged to make alliances between clans. If a wife died, her husband could remarry; but if a husband died, a widow could not marry. Children were raised according to strict Confucian ideas of family life.

The Korean aristocrats virtually became more Confucian (actually Neo-Confucian) than the Chinese themselves. They were so devoted to the thought of Zhu Xi that they were genuinely concerned when they learned that the philosophy of his opponent, Wang Yang-ming was being honored in Ming China. Wang Yang-ming believed that intuition was more important than study and investigation in determining the truth, and sought to make Confucianism a practical philosophy in everyday life by emphasizing the link of thought with action. They believed that this was a serious deviation from the truth.

Still, the Koreans accepted a proper and traditional "younger brother" relationship with China. Even at home the Korean ruler was referred to by the people as king, not emperor. The Yi kings accepted ordination at the hand of the Chinese Son of Heaven.

THE HANGUL SCRIPT

In adopting the principles of Confucianism, the kings of the Yi Dynasty (1392–1910) believed that they were adopting universal values that placed them in the civilized world. However the Yi saw themselves as custodians of the Korean identity as well. They developed their own script, called Hangul. Songs were composed in praise of the Yi house—Songs of the Flying Dragon. They praised the Yi and their ancestors whose virtues had brought them the Mandate of Heaven. The Yi are portrayed as more generous, modest, and committed to the Confucian ideal than their Chinese counterparts.

MILITARY TIES

Korea's bond to China was strengthened when Japan invaded Korea at the end of the 16th century. The Koreans called on China for help, and the Chinese came to their aid. However, the Ming dynasty of China was overthrown in 1644 by Manchu warriors from the north. The Manchus set up their own dynasty, called the Qing, a dynasty that would last until 1911. It was a shock to Koreans to realize that China was now ruled by "barbarians." The Koreans began to see their own nation as the repository of the true Confucian culture.

CONFUCIANISM COMES TO JAPAN

Chinese travelers during the Han dynasty provided the first written record of the Japanese, whom they called the people of Wa. Always concerned about family relations and proper behavior, the Chinese travelers were surprised to find different traditions among the Japanese: "In their meetings . . . there is no distinction between father and son or between men and women . . . In their worship men of importance simply clap their hands instead of kneeling or bowing."

Japanese clapped hands to summon or recognize the *kami*, spirits who the Japanese believed inhabited rocks, mountains, rivers—any extraordinary person or virtually any of the objects in nature. The *kami* are the "gods" of the indigenous Japanese religion, Shinto.

Over time visitors from China and Korea brought Confucianism, Daoism, and Buddhism to Japan, as well as the Chinese system of writing. Around the fifth century C.E. Chinese and Korean settlers acted as scribes for any writing needs. The early Japanese had no writing system of their own, and their system of government was based on clans. The Yamato clan claimed the greatest power, and its head was the emperor of Japan. According to Shinto myth the emperor was descended from the sun goddess, Amaterasu, the most powerful *kami* of all, and was thus divine.

PRINCE SHOKOTU TAISHI

Under the regency of Prince Shotoku Taishi (576–622), a prince of the Yomato family, steps were taken to make the new ideas part of Japan. Educated in a Buddhist monastery, Shotoku was devoted to that religion. Having learned to read and write Chinese, he became intrigued by other forms of Chinese learning. He believed that Confucianism provided great lessons for government and society. He hoped that Confucian principles would help to modernize Japan.

Prince Shotoku wanted to learn more about Chinese culture from the source. He sent a delegation of Japanese students to China. His initial efforts were met with a rebuff because he had used

In 604 Prince Shotoku of the Yomato family issued the Seventeen Articles Constitution, Japan's first written code of laws. Its general statement of principles described Buddhism as a universal truth for all living beings. In Article III the nature of the nation of Japan is presented in terms of Confucianism: "The lord is Heaven, the vassal is Earth. Heaven overspreads, Earth unbears. When this is so the four seasons follow their due course, and the owners of Nature develop their efficacy."

A Harmonious Universe

Confucianism was important for Japanese court etiquette and ceremony, but it did not sink deep roots among the people, as Buddhism did. There was one exception, however. The Confucianism that entered Japan was the Han variety, which incorporated belief in yin/yang forces (the two forces constantly influencing the universe, both continually changing in power and both necessary for balance) and the five elements (wood, metal, fire, water, and earth). These concepts became popular among Japanese, who liked the idea that the universe is a harmonious system in which people and nature continually interact.

an incorrect form of address in his letter to the Chinese emperor: "The Son of Heaven in the land where the sun rises [Japan] addresses a letter to the Son of Heaven where the sun sets [China]." Insulted, the Chinese court insisted that the letter be changed to one with due respect for the only Son of Heaven—and it was.

From Shotoku's time, the Japanese continued to seek out Chinese learning. Scholars read the "yellow rolls," or Chinese books, and studied the doctrines of Confucius. The descriptions of China's civilization inspired the Japanese to model their state on China. Using Confucian principles the Japanese reformers called for an emperor who would be in charge of the entire country, not just the first among the clan leaders. The emperor adopted the elaborate rituals of Confucianism to increase his grandeur. Court officials were grouped in ranks. A national university was founded to train Japanese in Confucian studies, Chinese literature, mathematics, and medicine. An examination system was begun to recruit talent.

In 710 Japan's first permanent capital was founded at Nara; it was a miniature version of the Chinese capital of Changan.

MAINTAINING JAPANESE IDENTITY

Japan did not adopt certain features of Confucianism. Japan was, and remained, an aristocratic society. Only members of the aristocratic class were permitted to take the examinations that led to government positions. The scholar never played as important a role in Japan as in China. Nor did the Japanese accept the Confucian idea of the Mandate of Heaven, for that implied the right to revolt against an unjust ruler, an idea that was abhorrent to the Japanese. In Japan the emperor was regarded as divine by birth. In Japanese history there would be only one dynasty, in contrast to the dynastic cycle of China.

NEO-CONFUCIANISM IN JAPAN

Confucianism reached its greatest influence in Japan after 1600. For the previous 400 years Japan had lacked a strong central government. In 1600 a powerful military leader, Tokugawa Ieyasu, defeated the last of his enemies and unified Japan under his control. He and his descendants ruled as shoguns, or military dictators. In theory the shoguns received their power from the emperor, who still carried on ancient rites. In reality the Tokugawa shoguns were the real rulers of Japan.

Two samurai fighting in a reenactment of a battle. Prior to 1600 great landowners, *daimyo,* and their warriors, samurai, fought for power and control of different parts of the country.

Up to this time Japan had remained in touch with China. It had absorbed the Neo-Confucian philosophy of Zhu Xi. The Tokugawa shoguns accepted this as the model for their state, for it promised stability and answered the need for a worldview that would promote order for the society.

FOUR CLASSES OF TOKUGAWA SOCIETY

Tokugawa Ieyasu was inspired by the second Tang emperor of China, Tai Zong, who ruled from 626 to 649. Tokugawa took his rule as a model to build stability and structure in his war-ravaged land. For advice he turned to the Japanese Neo-Confucian Hayashi Razan (1583–1657). Hayashi used Neo-Confucian theory to justify the division of Tokugawa society into four rigid classes: nobles and samurai (warriors), farmers, artisans, and merchants. (Although it was never rigidly enforced by the authorities, China too had such a division, with the scholar rather than the warrior on top.)

The Hayashi family became the official interpreters of Confucianism in Japan. At their urging Tokugawa shoguns built a Sage's Hall, where shoguns paid homage to an image of Confucius. The fifth shogun, a particularly enthusiastic and devout Confucian, constructed a Paragon Hall at the center of Edo (today's Tokyo), the capital of the shogunate. The shogun himself proudly gave a lecture there on the Confucian Classics. He also established a School of Prosperous Peace dedicated to Confucian studies, which became the cultural and educational center of Tokugawa Japan.

Universal Principles

Neo-Confucian Hayashi Razan (1583–1657) divided Japan into four classes: nobles and samurai (warriors), farmers, artisans, and merchants. He saw his highly ordered society as a reflection of universal principles. He wrote:

Heaven is above and earth is below. This is the order of heaven and earth. If we can understand the meaning of the order existing between heaven and earth, we can also perceive that in everything there is an order separating those who are above and those who are below. When we extend this understanding between heaven and earth, we cannot allow disorder in the relations between the ruler and the subject, and between those who are above and those who are below. The separation into four classes of samurai, farmers, artisans and merchants, like the five relationships, is part of the principles of heaven and is the Way which was taught by the Sage.

(In Conrad Totman, *Japan Before Perry.*)

KAIBARA EKKEN

The samurai scholar Kaibara Ekken (1630–1714) brought Neo-Confucianism into the homes of ordinary Japanese people. He set down in simple Japanese the basic moral principles of Confucianism. He described the proper forms of everyday conduct, the five relationships, duties within the family and toward feudal lords, and so forth. His writings made Confucian moral teachings "household talk" among the Japanese people. His guide to education advised parents: "Beginning [when a child is eight years old] teach the youngsters etiquette befitting their age and caution them not to commit an act of impoliteness."

Kaibara had been trained as a physician, which may have given him the more objective approach that distinguished him from scholars who pursued more abstruse forms of Neo-Confucian thought. He advised his readers: "Investigate things and make your knowledge perfect!" Other Neo-Confucians in Japan and China had concentrated their "investigation of things" on the Confucian classics. Kaibara took his own inquiries into the field of nature, producing works on farming, botany, and medicinal herbs. To Kaibara an understanding of nature was necessary for an understanding of human beings.

BUSHIDO

Historically the duty of the samurai had been to fight for their lord. However military action had no place under the Tokugawa shogunate, which sought to enforce peace within the society. Still the samurai felt a duty to practice their martial skills. Ironically Confucianism became part of the samurai code known as Bushido, or "way of the warrior." Yamago Soko (1622–85) developed the most important statement of Bushido's principles. Yamaga equated the samurai with the Confucian

The Way of the Warrior

Confucianism became part of the samurai code known as Bushido, or "the way (do) of the warrior (bushi)." Yamago Soko (1622–85) developed the most important statement of Bushido's principles:

Within his hearth he keeps to the ways of peace, but without he keeps his weapons ready for use. The three classes of the common people make him their teacher and respect him. By following his teachings, they are enabled to understand what is fundamental and what is secondary.

"gentleman" and taught that his essential function was to practice virtue as an example to the lower classes.

To Yamaga the most important of the Confucian virtues was righteousness, which he interpreted as an obligation or a duty. A samurai had to be ready to give up his life for duty. If duty required him to break the law or disobey government authority, the samurai would do it—and then prove his sincerity by committing suicide to atone for his crime against the government.

The main tower of Himeji Castle. A fort was first constructed on the site in 1333 but the five-storied main tower was constructed in 1581 by the son-in-law of the Shogun Ieyasu Tokogawa.

THE DIVINE LIGHT OF HEAVEN

Though the Tokugawa government supported the Neo-Confucianism of Zhu Xi, Zhu's opponent, Wang Yang-ming, also won adherents. Nakae Toju (1608–48) had studied Zhu Xi's writings for many years, but on discovering the work of Wang Yang-ming he became convinced that Wang's intuitive approach was superior to Zhu's rational "investigation of things." Nakae particularly stressed Wang's idea that in each person was an innate moral sense. This meant that one did not have to be a scholar to become a good person. Nakae called this inner sense the Divine Light of Heaven, and his teachings emphasized a personal god called the Supreme Lord Above. Nakae was also impressed by Wang's emphasis on action. Discussing or even understanding virtue were not sufficient; goodness had to be expressed in deeds.

Nakae practiced what he preached. After developing his philosophy he resigned his post in the service of a daimyo (landowner) and returned to his native village to care for his elderly mother. Though the village was in a remote region Nakae's fame as a teacher spread. While other Confucians generally wrote for scholars and officials, Nakae addressed the humblest people, both men and women. The popularity of Nakae's philosophy helped spread Confucianism as a form of religion in Japan.

AN INDEPENDENT NATION

Japan had a more independent relationship with China than Vietnam and Korea. Never conquered by a military force, protected by the Sea of Japan and the Tsushima Strait, which separated their country from mainland Asia, the Japanese avoided China's dominance. Over the centuries they stopped their tribute missions to the Chinese court.

Under the Tokugawa shogunate Japan isolated itself from the rest of the world. While retaining Neo-Confucianism as a state philosophy, the shoguns cut off relations with China altogether. Indeed, Japanese Confucians used the divine nature of their emperor and the fact that Japan had only one imperial family to portray Japan as more Confucian than China itself.

CHAPTER 5

CONFUCIAN LITERATURE

The Confucian Five Classics (*Book of Poetry, Book of History, Book of Rites, Book of Changes,* and *Spring and Autumn Annals*) hold a unique place in Chinese and east Asian civilization. The Chinese word for "classic," *jing,* can also be used to describe the "warp"—the threads that form the framework of a woven fabric. A *jing* was a work of a particular time (usually ancient) and place, whose truths were universal and timeless. Although the Chinese did not believe that the Five Classics were the revealed word of God, they believed that the wisdom contained in them could serve as a guide to people of all times. To the Chinese, the Five Classics were the "warp" of their civilization.

To the young Chinese student required to memorize them, the Five Classics were a vast collection of stories and precepts. They were not organized into disciplines or topics (except those implied by their titles), nor were they logically arranged. Instructions on how to dress and write poetry appeared side by side with injunctions to follow such virtues as patience and humility. The precepts, or advice on correct behavior, were phrased as moral

Students learning Confucian classics and traditional manners at a Confucian school in Chunghakdong village, Korea. The village has maintained a traditional lifestyle based on Confucianism for hundreds of years.

absolutes. It was understood that their authority came from their success in the past. Reading the Classics, the young scholar had to absorb their messages as clues to the one true way of life.

Because the Classics dealt with the past the Chinese tended to look on history as a model for behavior and truth. History and poetry became the two arts closely tied to Confucianism. From the time of the Han dynasty, when Confucianism became the official state religion under emperor Wu Di in 136 B.C.E., the Five Classics were studied by everyone who hoped to become a scholar or an official. Along with the *Analects*, written by Confucius's disciples shortly after his death, they have formed the cornerstone of Confucian thought for more than 2,000 years.

A POEM FROM THE BOOK OF POETRY

The following selection about music, nature, and war is an example of the poems included in the *Book of Poetry*, one of the Five Classics:

> The blind musicians
> In the courtyard of Chou
> Have set up their pillars and
>   crossbars
> With upright plumes and hooks for
>   the drumsand the bells;
> The small and large drums are
>   hanging there,
> The tambourines, the stone chimes,
>   the batons and tiger clappers.
> When all have been struck the
>   music begins;
> Then the pipes and the flutes
>   sound shrilly.
> Sweet is the music,
> Sweet as the song of birds.
> The ancestors listen;
> They are our guests;
> Forever and ever they gaze upon
>   our victories.

(In Elizabeth Seeger, *Eastern Religions*.)

THE FIVE CLASSICS

The Five Classics are the basic texts of Confucianism. They are revered because they are China's oldest literature and, according to tradition, because Confucius edited them. He referred to some of them in his teaching. Modern scholars think that the duke of Zhou (r. 1043–1036 B.C.E.), a great figure of the early Zhou dynasty and Confucius's ideal ruler, may have written some parts of them. Certainly parts of the Five Classics come from very ancient times, although the texts as they exist today have been added to and modified through the centuries since Confucius lived.

BOOK OF POETRY

The *Shijing* contains the oldest Chinese poetry. It is a collection of more than three hundred poems—sometimes called songs because early Chinese poetry was sung.

Over half of the poems describe experiences common to all people—love, work, and war. The rest are court poems, including praise of the founders of the Zhou dynasty and hymns used in sacrificial rites. Confucius, who loved to sing, is reputed to have selected the poems for the book. He urged his students to memorize them and he used them in his teaching.

BOOK OF RITES

This book consists of three separate ritual texts: the *Zhou Li*, or *Rites of Zhou*, which describes the bureaucratic system of the Zhou dynasty; the *Yi Li*, or *Ceremonial*, which contains descriptions of the etiquette of events in the life of the aristocracy such as weddings, banquets, sacrifices, funerals, and archery contests; and the *Liji*, or *Book of Rites*. This is the longest of the three ritual texts, describing government regulations as well as providing instructions on how to manage a household, cook, behave at a dinner party or a funeral, drive a carriage, name a baby, and conduct oneself in everyday life.

The *Book of Rites* as it exists today is not the one that Confucius himself studied. It contains a varied collection of stories and essays compiled during the Han dynasty from earlier writings, including many stories about Confucius's own life. These stories often describe Confucius's comments on ancient sacrifices, reinterpreting them for a more enlightened age. For example, before Confucius the ancient Chinese believed that by having a living person ascend to the roof of the house and call for the dead to return, the spirits of the dead could be summoned back to their bodies. Objects buried with the dead were originally intended to be used by them in an afterlife. Confucian scholars of Han times wrote that those objects merely symbolized the wishes of the living that the dead person could be called back to life. The

Court Rituals

Parts of the *Book of Rites* deal with proper ceremonial form, and they became a handbook for the emperor's court. One passage declares that if the emperor wore white instead of red (the summer color) in the last month of summer disasters would follow. "High ground would be flooded, the grain in the fields would not ripen, and there would be many miscarriages among women."

Book of Rites today describes Confucius as saying: "To treat the dead as dead would show a lack of love and therefore cannot be done; to treat the dead as living would show a lack of wisdom and likewise cannot be done." Thus the ritual texts describe ways of paying respect to the departed and regulating the emotions of the living so that grief will be appropriate.

BOOK OF HISTORY

The *Shujing* is the oldest source of Chinese mythology and history, beginning with the legendary emperors who brought the tools of

FROM THE BOOK OF HISTORY

The following selection is from the earliest section of the *Book of History* and concerns the reign of the legendary emperor Yao. The selection describes how the emperor chose a farmer, Shun, over his own son, Chu, because of Shun's virtue and filial piety. Yao and Shun were paragons of Confucian virtue.

The Emperor said (to his advisors): "You must (make a calendar that will) fix the four seasons and complete the year . . . Who will carefully attend to this? I will raise him up and employ him." Fang Chi [one of his advisors] said: "Your heir-son Chu is enlightened." The emperor said: "Alas, he is deceitful and quarrelsome . . . Promote someone who is already illustrious, or raise up someone who is humble and mean." They all said to the emperor: "There is an unmarried man in a low position called Shun of Yu." The emperor said: "Yes, I

have heard of him. What is he like?" The Chief said: "He is the son of a blind man. His father is stupid, his mother is deceitful, his half brother Hsiang is arrogant. Yet he has been able to live in harmony with them and to be splendidly filial. He has controlled himself and has not come to wickedness." The emperor said, "I will try him; I will (give him my two daughters as wives) and observe his behavior towards (them)." He gave orders and sent down his two daughters to the bend of the Kuei River to be wives in the House of Yu. The emperor said: "Be reverent."

Shun of Yu, according to the text, proved so able at his task that the emperor Yao abdicated and let him ascend the throne.

(In William Theodore DeBary, *Sources of Chinese Tradition*.)

A Taiwanese man dressed as Confucius hands out cards to children on which Confucian teachings have been written. This special event was held in Taipei on the island of Taiwan to promote Confucian values and teachings among the public.

civilization to the Chinese. The text continues through the Xia, Shang, and early Zhou dynasties (so roughly covering from ca. 2070 B.C.E. to ca. 256 B.C.E.). It was one of the books that Qin Shi Huangdi destroyed in 213 B.C.E. when legalists persuaded him that the Confucians were his enemies. By tradition scholars of his time preserved it in memory, and it was rewritten during the Han dynasty (206 B.C.E.–220 C.E.). The book is sometimes called the *Book of Documents,* and Confucius himself referred to it that way. This is a more accurate description of its contents, which include decrees, speeches, advice from counselors, and similar reports on government affairs. The Chinese regarded history as the mirror of the present and important in Chinese education and thought; by studying the past one could learn lessons useful for the present.

SPRING AND AUTUMN ANNALS

The *Chun Qiu* is a brief chronicle of the events in Confucius's home state of Lu between the years 722 B.C.E. and 481 B.C.E. The term *spring and autumn* is a shortened form of *spring, summer, autumn, winter*. The officials of the state of Lu compiled it as a season-by-season record of events. Because the end date comes so close to the death of Confucius his followers have often asserted that he was the actual author, using earlier records in the state archives. The text is cryptic and difficult to understand and has been the subject of many commentaries dating back as far as the early Han dynasty.

BOOK OF CHANGES

The *Yijing* is a book of divination that helps its followers predict future events and understand human existence and natural occurrences. The book consists of 64 "hexagrams" (each being a combination of six broken or unbroken lines) with accompanying interpretations. Later writers added a series of appendices that give further interpretations. Confucius is said to have written some of this material, but this is doubtful. Only once in the *Analects* does he refer to the *Yijing*: "Give me a few years and by 50 I shall have studied the book of divination called Changes. Through it I may become free of large faults."

By throwing coins or by manipulating sticks of the yarrow (a plant with magical properties) a petitioner selects any one or two of the hexagrams, and the accompanying text opens up the questioner's prospects or gives guidance. The 64 hexagrams are formed by a combination of any two of the eight "trigrams" (figures made with three horizontal lines, broken or unbroken) representing Heaven, Thunder, Water, Mountain, Earth, Wind, Fire, and Lake.

Through the ages the *Yijing* has escaped destruction during book burnings and has enjoyed wide appeal in China, Japan, and more recently in the West as a fortune-telling manual and an aid to meditation and reflection.

The *Yijing* filled a need in Confucian thought that was not met by the other Classics. Early Confucian scholars were concerned with ethical and political problems. However the *Yijing* provided a mystical key to the workings of the universe. Later scholars wrote countless volumes linking its messages to Confucian thought. It helped to make Confucianism an appealing alternative to Daoism, which was greatly concerned with mysticism and magic.

THE FOUR BOOKS

Zhu Xi, the Neo-Confucian thinker of the Song dynasty (960–1279 C.E.), was particularly impressed by two sections of the *Book of Rites*. He assembled these sections into books now called the *Great Learning* and the *Doctrine of the Mean*. To give them added significance Zhu Xi made these two books part of what he called the Four Books. The other two are the *Analects,* the sayings of Confucius; and the *Meng Zi,* or *Mencius,* which contains the teachings of the greatest figure in Confucianism after the sage himself.

Through the influence of the Neo-Confucians, the Four Books became the basis of Chinese education. A student had to memorize them before beginning the study of the Five Classics. From 1313 to 1905 the Four Books were the basis of the examination system that produced officials for China's government.

THE ULTIMATE SOURCE

The first hexagram in the *Yijing*, the book of divination that helps its followers foretell future events, is formed with six unbroken lines. The book names this hexagram *tien*, the Ultimate Source. It means great success. The commentary reads, in part:

Great indeed is tien, the ultimate source. The ten thousand things receive their beginnings from it. It governs Heaven. The clouds drift by and the rain falls. All things flow into their forms. The ends and the beginnings are greatly illuminated. The six lines of the hexagram take shape at their own times. In timely fashion they ride the six dragons and so rule over the heavens. The way of tien is change and transformation. Each thing thereby achieves its true nature and destiny and assures that it is in accord with great harmony. There is great benefit and constancy . . .

(In William Theodore DeBary, *Sources of Chinese Tradition*.)

ANALECTS

The *Analects* in its present form was probably composed by the second generation of Confucius's disciples. They wrote down what they heard from those who had actually known Confucius.

The *Analects* consists of 497 verses, some very brief. Nowhere does Confucius discuss philosophical principles or detailed regulations for a way of life. He merely comments on a specific problem or situation and suggests a proper reaction.

The *Analects* has served as a guide to life for hundreds of millions, perhaps billions, of people in the 2,500 years since it was written. Generations of students memorized the entire book as the first stage in their education. They were not expected to understand it fully, but by committing it to memory they would create in their minds a storehouse of thought that would deepen in significance as they grew older. They could spend the rest of their lives pondering its meaning and discovering how it applied to their own lives. According to the personal testimony of those who did this, the book takes on greater significance as one grows older and experiences life. Through young adulthood, middle age,

Students and their teacher play a balancing game while taking a break from studying Confucian classics and learning about traditional values and duties at a Confucian school in Chunghakdong, Korea.

EXCERPTS FROM THE *ANALECTS*

The *Analects* gives insight into the wisdom of Great Master Kong. Read the following to gain a flavor of its scope and philosophy.

Clever talk and a domineering manner have little to do with being man-at-his-best.

While his father lives, observe a man's purposes; when the father dies, observe his actions. If for three years (of mourning) a man does not change from the ways of his father, he may be called filial.

At fifteen I thought only of study; at thirty I began playing my role; at forty I was sure of myself; at fifty I was conscious of my position in the universe; at sixty I was no longer argumentative; and now at seventy I can follow my heart's desire without violating custom.

While the parents live, serve them according to the rites. When they die, bury them according to the rites and make the offerings to them according to the rites.

Look at the means which a man employs, consider his motives; observe his pleasures. A man simply cannot conceal himself.

Learning without thought brings ensnarement. Thought without learning totters.

Shall I tell you what knowledge is? It is to know both what one knows and what one does not know.

A hamlet of ten homes will surely contain someone as loyal and reliable as I, but none to equal my love of learning.

To take note of things in silence, to retain curiosity despite much study, never to weary of teaching others: no one surpasses me in these three things.

I do not instruct the uninterested; I do not help those who fail to try. If I mention one corner of a subject and the pupil does not deduce therefrom the other three, I drop him.

When the Master heard in Ch'i a melody ascribed to the great sage Shun, he went three months without meat. "I never thought so fine a melody had ever been composed!"

The Master used the pronunciation of the capital when reciting The Poems and The Writings of Old, and also when pronouncing the rites.

Study as if you were never to master it, as if in fear of losing it.

and old age one comes to understand Confucius's words more fully and appreciate their importance. This is why this book has remained one of the most widely read texts in world civilization.

The following sample passages from the *Mencius* show that Mencius, the second great thinker in the Confucian tradition, regarded political power as flowing upward from the people, not downward from the ruler. For this reason, parts of the *Mencius* were suppressed by the government at various times in Chinese history.

Mencius said: "Men are in the habit of speaking of the world, the state. As a matter of fact, the foundation of the world lies in the state, the foundation of the state lies in the family, and the foundation of the family lies in the individual." Mencius said: "(In the constitution of a state) the people rank the highest, the spirits of land and grain come next, and the ruler counts the least." Mencius said to King Hsuan of Chi: "When the ruler regards the ministers as his hands and feet, the ministers regard their ruler as their heart and bowels. When the ruler regards his ministers as his dogs and horses, the ministers regard their ruler as a stranger. When the ruler regards his ministers as dust and grass, the ministers regard their ruler as a brigand or foe."

(In William Theodore DeBary, *Sources of Chinese Tradition.*)

MENG ZI (MENCIUS)

Mencius's disciples probably set down his teachings in writing not long after his death. Though the *Mencius* is similar in form to the *Analects*, the passages in the *Mencius* are typically much longer than those in the *Analects*. The book reflects the fact that Confucianism faced many intellectual challenges in Mencius's time. The view of a competing philosopher is often cited, and Mencius gives his detailed refutation of it. He also comments on specific sayings of Confucius, giving his own views on their significance and meaning. The *Mencius* shows the "second sage" to be a more argumentative person than Confucius. Frequently he argues with the rulers of his time, pointing out clearly the error of their ways.

Confucius's doctrine, in its various forms, was often popular with rulers because it demanded that the subjects revere their ruler as they did their fathers. It was easy to overlook the underlying idea that loyalty was a two-way affair. The ruler must also govern with justice and wisdom. Mencius put much greater stress on this side of Confucian teaching.

GREAT LEARNING

According to tradition the *Great Learning* is a section of the *Book of Rites* written by

Confucius's grandson. Though Confucius's own son was a disappointment as he did not prove to be a consistent student, his grandson became an important teacher who helped to carry on the sage's doctrine.

The *Great Learning* is a kind of guide to becoming a true Confucian gentleman. Its theme is self-cultivation. For centuries young boys and men studied it to learn how to follow the Confucian way in their own lives. It is, however, more than a guide to self-improvement. The *Great Learning* was addressed to the emperor and to the officials who served him (as well as those who aspired to become officials). Thus self-cultivation was carried out for the ultimate goal of good government. It rests on the Confucian idea that before a man can regulate others he must learn to regulate himself.

An anonymous 10th-century Chinese painting, *Banquet and Concert,* which depicts elegant ladies of the Tang imperial court enjoying a feast and music. Following Confucian traditions, ladies were generally excluded from serious matters of court.

DOCTRINE OF THE MEAN

The Chinese title of the *Doctrine of the Mean, Zhong Yong,* consists of the characters for *normality* and *centrality* and conveys the Confucian ideas of moderation, balance, and harmony. The work consists of a series of essays and stories. Some describe the character and duties of a true gentleman, the performance of social obligations, and the duties of rulers. Others are quotations from

LESSONS FOR WOMEN

Ban Zhao, court historian from the Han period (206 B.C.E.–220 C.E.), described in her text, *Lessons for Women,* how females were treated from birth in Chinese society:

> On the third day after the birth of a girl the ancients observed three customs: (first) to place the baby below the bed; (second) to give her a potsherd with which to play; and (third) to announce her birth to her ancestors by an offering. Now to lay the baby below the bed plainly indicated that she is lowly and weak, and should regard it as her primary duty to humble herself before others. To give her potsherds with which to play indubitably signified that she should practice labor and consider it her primary duty to be industrious. To announce her birth before her ancestors clearly meant that she ought to esteem as her primary duty the continuation of the observance of worship in the home . . . Let a woman retire late to bed, but rise early to duties; let her not dread tasks by day or by night. Let her not refuse to perform domestic duties whether easy or difficult. That which must be done, let her finish completely, tidily, and systematically. Then she may be said to be industrious . . . Yet only to teach men and not to teach women—is that not ignoring the essential relation between them? According to the (Book of) Rites, it is the rule to begin to teach (male) children to read at the age of eight years, and by the age of fifteen years they ought then to be ready for cultural training. Only why should it not be (that girls' education as well as boys' be) according to this principle?

(In Nancy Lee Swann, *Pan Chao, Foremost Woman Scholar of China.*)

Confucius or accounts of his discussions with rulers and disciples.

The "mean" praised in this work is the "normal" course of human action, which could bring harmony to the world if sincerely followed. The *Zhong Yong* reads: "The life of the gentleman is an exemplification of the Mean; the life of the inferior man is a contradiction of it. (The gentleman) constantly holds to the center. (The inferior man) knows no restraint."

CONFUCIAN INSTRUCTIONS FOR WOMEN

Confucianism reflected the male-dominated Chinese society. All the emperor's scholar-officials were male, and only males could take the examinations that led to government service. However, through the force of her ability, Ban Zhao (ca. 45–120 C.E.) obtained the position (though not the title) of court historian to the Han emperor Ho. Ban Zhao's work became the official history of the period, preserved through the centuries by later dynasties. She was the only woman in Chinese history to obtain such an important post.

In addition Ban Zhao was in charge of the education of the young empress and her ladies-in-waiting. In this position she wrote a text called *Lessons for Women*. It is the earliest work from any world civilization to deal with women's education. Ban Zhao was a Confucian and she accepted the Confucian view of the role of women. Yet in her work she allowed herself a plea for women's equality in education.

Ban Zhao—
Unofficial Court Historian

Ban Zhao came from an illustrious family. The name Ban means "tiger." According to tradition one of her ancestors was born the illegitimate son of a royal family member. He was abandoned and was suckled by a female tiger until his grandparents rescued him. Ban Zhao's father, Ban Piao, began to write a history of China, but he died before he could finish it. One of his sons, Ban Gu, took up the task. Ban Gu also wrote the first book on the game of chess. Ban Gu was imprisoned when he became involved in political intrigue, however. Meanwhile Gu's twin brother, Ban Chao, made a name for himself as a military leader. The emperor sent him to the Tarim Basin in the western part of the empire. There Ban Chao subdued barbarian tribesmen and secured China's hold on the region. Early in her life Ban Zhao had married, but when her husband died she returned to her parents' home. Using the extensive family library she began to study and write. When the emperor heard of her accomplishments he called on her to finish the history that her father and brother had begun. The history that the Bans wrote became a model for later writers. Traditionally the scholars of each dynasty would write the official history of the dynasty that preceded it.

QUALITIES OF A SAMURAI

Yamaga Soko (1622–85), known in Japan as one of the three greatest samurai (warriors) of the Tokugawa shogunate, presented the qualities required of a samurai in the terms of Confucian philosophy:

> The business of the samurai consists in reflecting on his own station in life, in discharging loyal service to his master if he has one, in deepening his fidelity (to) friends, and, with due consideration of his own position, in devoting himself to duty above all. However, in one's own life, one becomes unavoidably involved in obligations between father and child, older and younger brother, and husband and wife. Though these are also the fundamental moral obligations of everyone in the land, the farmers, artisans, and merchants have no leisure from their occupations, and so they cannot constantly act in accordance with them and fully exemplify the Way. The samurai dispenses with the business of the farmer, artisan, and merchant and confines himself to practicing this Way; should there be someone in the three classes of the common people who transgresses against these moral principles, the samurai summarily punishes him and thus upholds proper moral principles in the land. It would not do for the samurai to know the martial and civil virtues without manifesting them. Since this is the case, outwardly he stands in physical readiness for any call to service and inwardly he strives to fulfill the Way of the lord and subject, friend and friend, father and son, older and younger brother, and husband and wife. Within his heart he keeps to the ways of peace, but without he keeps his weapons ready for use. The three classes of the common people make him their teacher and respect him. By following his teachings, they are enabled to understand what is fundamental and what is secondary.
>
> (In Patricia Buckley Ebrey (editor), *Chinese Civilization and Society*.)

A traditional Samurai helmet being worn during the re-enactment of a feudal battle between rival samurai. The samurai were a Japanese warrior class working for military leaders during the period of the Shoguns who divided Japan into feudal territories. The code of these Japanese warriors was influenced by Confucian duties, responsibilities and rituals.

A CONFUCIAN CODE FOR A WARRIOR

Yamaga Soko (1622–85) is known in Japan as one of the three greatest samurai of the Tokugawa shogunate. As a young man he gained respect because of his knowledge of Shinto, Buddhism, Daoism, and Neo-Confucianism. Many samurai of the time turned to scholarship, for there was no need for their military skills in a Japan that was unified under the shogun. Yamaga taught many others, including the leader of the 47 *ronin*, a group of samurai whose selfless dedication to duty has inspired countless Japanese stories and plays.

Yamaga set down the first systematic description of Bushido, the Japanese "way of the warrior." This code required a life of austerity and self-discipline. It included a readiness to meet death at any time.

The 47 Ronin

When samurai (warrior) Yamaga Soto (1622–85) was the military instructor for the daimyo (lord) of Ako, he taught the future leader of the 47 *ronin*. This was a band of samurai whose master had been forced to commit *seppuku,* or suicide, after an incident at the shogun's court. The *ronin* (masterless samurai) pledged to avenge his death, and after carrying out their plot against the enemy of their master they too committed suicide. Countless Japanese stories and plays have celebrated the 47 *ronin's* selfless dedication to duty.

CHAPTER 6

RITUALS AND STANDARDS OF CONDUCT

On the night before the winter solstice the Chinese emperor prepared for the most important ceremony of the year. The gates of the Forbidden City, where the emperor and his family lived, were thrown open. The emperor climbed into a sedan chair (a portable chair, borne on poles) that was draped with cloths embroidered with golden dragons and, carried by 16 nobles, began his procession south. Two thousand people, including princes, ministers, officials, and servants in colorful uniforms, led the way through the great capital city. The path they followed had been sprinkled with gold sand. Flag bearers carried banners of the 28 constellations, the five planets, and the five sacred mountains. Finally the procession passed through the southern gate of the capital city, the seat of government, and moved on to the four-mile-square grounds of the Temple of Heaven.

Inside the grounds the emperor visited the memorial tablets of his ancestors. Then he retired to the Hall of Fasting, where he purified himself in preparation for his duties the next day. Before

In the Forbidden City of Beijing, tourists now explore where once Chinese emperors lived apart from the ordinary citizens beyond the palace walls. Court and government life centered around the Forbidden City and followed the emperor when he moved to his summer palace outside the city.

dawn he emerged from the hall and went to a triple-tiered marble altar that stood open to the sky. Nothing was allowed to stand between the altar and Heaven. There the emperor would perform the annual ceremonies to renew his reign's Mandate of Heaven.

IMPERIAL CEREMONIES AT THE TEMPLE OF HEAVEN

The ceremony followed ancient tradition. The emperor, clad in dragon-embroidered blue robes and wearing a bonnet with pearl tassels, ascended the steps to the altar—circular in shape like Heaven—and lighted a pile of sticks. The smoke that rose invited Heaven to take part in the ceremony. Then the emperor laid on the altar incense, rolls of blue silk, and disks of blue jade. The chief sacrificial victim was a young bull free from any blemish. It had been slaughtered and cooked the night before. The emperor took a piece of the meat and laid it before the throne. He placed other pieces at his ancestors' tablets, which had been placed alongside. Prostrating himself nine times in farewell, he descended the altar steps and, as he watched from below, the offerings were burned in blue cups and bowls.

The main structure of the Temple of Heaven, south of Beijing. Here the emperor performed the ceremonies that renewed the Mandate of Heaven that gave him the authority to reign as the Son of Heaven.

While the emperor was carrying out those duties the sounds of flutes, gongs, and musical stones echoed around the altar. Dancers performed the precise movements that were a part of the ceremony. Century after century, from ancient times until 1916, this scene remained virtually the same—at different capitals, under different dynasties, in peace and in war. The forms and details of this ritual remained unchanged because they were set down in the *Book of Rites,* one of the Confucian Five Classics. The book states firmly, "The wise kings of old knew that the rules of ceremony could not be dispensed with, while the ruin of states, the destruction of families and the punishing of individuals are always preceded by the abandonment of these rules." Literally the whole country's welfare depended on the emperor's carrying out these rites in the proper form. His duty was to ensure that human affairs be kept in perfect harmony with the Will of Heaven. Only he, the Son of Heaven, could perform them.

The winter solstice ceremony carried out by the emperor marked the return to power of the yang force, which symbolizes the visible heaven and the sun after the yin winter of cold and darkness. At the summer solstice the emperor performed a similar rite on the north side of the capital—the direction of earth, on which all life depends. Because yang had reached the height of its power, it was time to turn the balance-wheel and honor yin. The northern altar was square, the shape of earth, and the predominant color of the emperor's ceremonial robes, the offerings, and the vessels used was yellow. In addition the offerings were buried in the earth, not burned.

THE THREE SACRIFICES

The sacrifices of state Confucianism were divided into Great, Medium, and Small. A government department, the Board of Rites, provided officials who guided all the participants, from emperor to musicians, through their duties. The emperor himself could delegate others to perform the Small and Medium rites. In fact his officials regularly performed such rites at temples of the state religion in the capitals of provinces, prefectures, and counties throughout the empire. Among the Medium sacrifices were those offered to Confucius in temples dedicated to his honor.

One of the Medium sacrifices was, however, customarily performed by the emperor at the Temple of Agriculture, southwest of the capital. At the beginning of the agricultural year, as Chinese farmers planted their crops, the emperor plowed six furrows in a sacred field. Princes and high officials plowed additional furrows. The empress performed yet another ceremony at an altar dedicated to the wife of Huang Di, the Yellow Emperor. Huang Di's wife was considered the patroness of silkworms because according to legend she had discovered the process of silk making.

TEMPLES AT QUFU

The largest and most important Confucian temple was at Confucius's family home in Qufu. By the time of the Ming dynasty (1368–1644) the sacred site occupied 49 acres, including several hundred halls and pavilions containing statues and pillars carved with the sage's words and praise for them. The heart of this complex is the Dacheng Dian, or Great Hall of Confucius. A short path leads through rows of trees to the entrance. The lower of its two roofs is supported by 10 marble pillars. Around each pillar carved dragons slide through puffs of clouds. Golden dragons recline on the blue beams that support the roof. Inside stand statues of Confucius, four companions who followed him in his wanderings, and 12 other disciples. Ceremonies take place in this Great Hall on Confucius's birthday (September 28) and in each season of the year. For centuries pilgrims have come to the awesome site to worship Confucius and ask his help with exams, promotions, troubles with children, and so forth.

The dragon is a powerful symbol in Chinese mythology and legend tells how dragons stood guard at the birth of Confucius.

THE EMPEROR'S SACRIFICES

There were four Great Sacrifices that only the emperor could perform. In addition to those to heaven and earth there was one to the dynastic ancestors and one to the gods of soil and grain. These sacrifices had been carried out since long before the time of Confucius, but over the centuries they had become part of the Confucian system. These were never public ceremonies; only those who had a specific role to play in a ritual were permitted to be present. The *Book of Rites* prescribed other ceremonies for times of unusual misfortunes, such as flood, famine, drought, or war. Though officials versed in the *Book of Rites* served as masters of ceremony to assist the emperor, they were not regarded as priests.

CULT OF CONFUCIUS

The sacrifices to Confucius took three forms. First, from the time of his death, his own descendants had carried out ancestral rites to him at the family home at Qufu in Lu, in today's Shandong province. Then when Confucius became the patron saint of the scholar class, all institutions of learning developed rituals to him. And last, as Confucius' teachings became entrenched in the state religion, he was honored as the most illustrious of China's sages.

During the Han dynasty (206 B.C.E.–220 C.E.), the scholar-officials encouraged the building of temples to Confucius throughout the empire. It seemed appropriate to honor him as the founder of the state religion and as a god, although there were always Confucian scholars who resisted the tendency to deify the sage.

TEMPLE OF CONFUCIUS IN BEIJING

The great temple of Confucius in Beijing, second only to the one at Confucius's family home in Qufu, was begun in 1273 and completed in 1306. The actual temple holds tablets of wood, some of them gilded, inscribed with the names of Confucius and his disciples. Outside in the grounds stand scores if not hundreds of stone steles with the details of those who came first in the imperial examination—with full records of their lineage and achieve-

The Book of Family Rituals

The Neo-Confucian Zhu Xi who lived from 1130 to 1200 wrote an immensely influential book called *Family Rituals*. It contained forms of liturgy for the home. In preparing his work Zhu Xi drew on traditional sources but modified them for simplicity's sake. His goal was to eliminate practices that he thought were vulgar or superstitious. In later centuries foreign travelers noted that virtually every home in China possessed a copy of Zhu Xi's book. From the 13th to the 20th century it served as a household guide to ritual and belief. It was also used in Vietnam, Korea, and Japan.

ments. The building has been rebuilt many times since the 14th century.

On certain days in the second and eighth months of the lunar year ceremonies took place in honor of the sage. They began with the striking of a great bell at about three o'clock in the morning. A master of ceremonies guided the participants through the ornate and complicated rites. With genuflections and prayers offerings of grain, fruit, oil, wine, jade, and silk were presented. One of the features of the ceremonies was music, for Confucius was particularly fond of it. An orchestra dressed in the costumes of the Ming court (1368–1644) played ancient instruments. A choir sang poetry composed for the occasion and rows of dancers holding feather wands solemnly performed steps that had been hallowed by tradition. This ceremony was the model for countless others held at the Confucian temples in other places.

FAMILY RITUALS

The emperor himself was the chief priest of the nation. Yet each household in the nation, even the humblest, had another "priest"—the father of the family that lived within. While Confucian ritual dominated, this was almost always interwoven with Daoist and/or Buddhist rituals, especially for births and deaths. The Chinese had paid special reverence to their ancestors long before the time of Confucius. Tablets with the ancestors' names were kept in shrines. It was the duty of the father to make sacrifices and report family matters to these shrines. He might sometimes be assisted by his eldest son or his wife, but only he could actually address the ancestors by name.

Rural villages often had a shrine for the families of the locality. Larger homes typically contained an offering hall to the east of the main room of the house. In the offering hall were four altars holding wooden tablets bearing the names of the ancestors. Each morning the head of the household visited the hall to report on family matters. The offering hall was also used for events such as a marriage or a child's reaching adulthood.

The forms of these family rituals varied at different times and places. All, however, followed the general practices of Confucian thought. In general the higher a family's status the more likely they were to carry out the elaborate forms prescribed in the *Book of Rites* and similar books.

NEWBORN CHILDREN

One of the Five Classics, the *Shijing*, or *Book of Poetry*, contains two poems describing how to treat newborns. This one of the poems:

So he bears a son,
And puts him to sleep upon a bed,
Clothes him in robes,
Gives him a jade scepter to play with.
The child's howling is very lusty;
In red greaves (leg armor) shall he flare,
Be lord and king of house and home.
Then he bears a daughter,
And puts her upon the ground,
Clothes her in swaddling clothes,
Gives her a loom-whorl to play with.
For her no decorations, no emblems;
Her only care the wine and food,
And how to give no trouble to father and mother.

(In Arthur Waley (translator), *The Book of Songs*.)

CHILDHOOD

As soon as possible children were taught to show proper behavior and respect for their elders. Zhu Xi's book advises parents: "Children old enough to eat should be given food and taught to use their right hands in eating. Those old enough to talk should be taught their names and greetings such as 'At your service,' 'Bless you,' and 'Sleep well.' Anytime they fail to behave properly toward (their seniors) they must be scolded and warned not to act that way again."

When children were six they were taught the words for numbers and directions. "Boys should begin learning how to write, and girls should be taught simple women's work." Both boys and girls learned to recite the *Analects*. By the time they were nine boys were reciting other books of the Confucian Five Classics. For

Children playing outside a Chinese village. Long before Confucius's time the Chinese valued male children more than females. This is was deeply ingrained cultural attitude that survives to this day. The different treatment of boys and girls began at birth.

girls the books *Biographies of Admirable Women* by Liu Hsiang and Han court historian Ban Zhao's *Education for Women* were recommended. At 10 boys went to a school outside the home but girls remained at home, taking "instruction in compliance and obedience and the principal household tasks." Those tasks included breeding silkworms, weaving, sewing, and cooking. Study of such things taught a girl "the hardships through which food and clothing are obtained so that she will not dare to be extravagant."

COMING OF AGE

A boy's becoming a man and a girl's becoming a woman were occasions for special ceremonies. The ceremony for a boy was usually celebrated when he was between the ages of 15 and 20. Three days before the ceremony the boy's father invited another man to be the sponsor. At dawn on the day of the event three sets of caps and robes were set out, and the participants assembled at the offering hall or the village shrine.

The head of the family entered first, followed in order of age by witnesses to the ceremony. Inside thc hall the sponsor placed the cap on the boy's head, and the boy went to a side room to don his long gown and shoes. The ceremony was repeated twice more with other garments such as a leather belt and boots. The sponsor then gave the boy his adult name. Afterward the boy's father presented him to the elders of the village as a full-fledged adult.

For a girl a similar ceremony took place when she became engaged, usually between the ages of 14 and 20. The girl's mother was the presiding woman, and once more a sponsor was invited. The sponsor placed a pin in the girl's hair and placed a woman's cap on her head. The girl then put on adult clothing and received a new name. Ceremonies for both boys and girls were followed by parties at the young person's home, at which the sponsor was guest of honor.

MARRIAGE

Children had virtually no say in the choice of a husband or wife. The parents on both sides made the decision and began negotiations through an intermediary. The decision was important to the groom's family, for it meant the arrival of a new member in its household. A suitable match was of equal importance to the bride's family, because if the marriage failed the bride would be returned to the family. The bride's family was expected to give a dowry, a gift of money or property, to the family of the groom.

The ancestors of each family were consulted, and after the intermediary had negotiated the dowry the groom's father made a report at his ancestors' shrine. He then had a younger brother of the groom take the written betrothal agreement to the bride's family. The bride's family entertained the messenger, and the bride's father took the document to his ancestors' shrine.

MARRIAGE RITUALS

Neo-Confucian Zhu Xi's book, *Family Rituals*, contains intricate formulas and explanations for all the marriage rites. For example when the groom visits his bride's family home after the marriage, her father must greet him at the doorway. Zhu Xi wrote that the groom "bows, then kneels, then takes (the father's) hand. They enter, and he is presented to his wife's mother. She is standing inside the left door to the inner quarters. The groom bows outside the door. All parties give gifts of silk." The groom has not previously met the bride's mother or other relatives or been served wine and food in their home. "The reason," explains Zhu Xi, "is that the bride has not yet been presented to her parents-in-law."

The day before the wedding the bride's family sent messengers to lay out the dowry in the groom's chamber. On the wedding day the groom went on horseback to the bride's home. Her father made a final report to the ancestors and then instructed his daughter as to her duties. The groom, bringing the traditional present of a goose, was invited into the house. The bride entered a carriage, usually decorated with red, the traditional bridal color, and the groom led the way to his house. There the two young people were honored with a feast. No priest or official pronounced them husband and wife. By exchanging cups of wine they made themselves a married couple.

The spirit of the ceremony was the shifting of the bride from her family to the groom's family. The day after the feast the bride was presented officially to her in-laws. If she was the wife of the eldest son she served her in-laws their food, a duty that would continue as long as her new mother and father lived. On the third day after the wedding the bride was presented at the ancestral shrine of her new family. The day after that the groom again visited his bride's family, who entertained him.

FILIAL PIETY

The family unit remained together for life. It was rare for a young couple to establish their own home. As long as the bride's parents-in-law lived she had to serve them with humility and respect. However, the same was true for the sons of the family. They had to greet their parents, using suitable phrases, each morning and evening.

The Dream of the Red Chamber

One of the greatest Chinese novels, *The Dream of the Red Chamber*, portrays the influence of Confucianism on an upper-class family. Written in the 18th century by Cao Queqin, the novel tells the story of the Jias, a large extended family. The central character, Jia Baoyu, is utterly dominated by his father. Baoyu fears his father's anger so much that just thinking of it causes him to quake with fear. Baoyu's mother is a powerless figure, but his grandmother, the mother of his father, commands respect because of her position as the oldest living member of the family. It is taken for granted that Baoyu must devote himself to the Confucian studies that will enable him to pass the imperial examinations. Baoyu is in love with one of his cousins, but his grandmother and father trick him into marrying another woman. At the novel's end, however, when Baoyu has passed the highest level of the examinations, he abandons his wife and family to become a monk.

Even as adults they had to inform their parents when they were leaving the house. If the children invited friends to the house they could not entertain them in the main room, which was reserved for parents. Zhu Xi wrote, "In his service to his parents, a son should like what his parents like and respect whomever his parents respect. This holds even for dogs and horses, so of course even more for people."

Then, as now, there were some children whose behavior did not reach the proper standard. Zhu Xi advised those parents, "Should their son or daughter-in-law not be respectful or filial, the parents should not try to take an immediate dislike. Instead they should teach him or her. If he or she remains intractable, they should try rebukes. If there is still no improvement, they should try flogging. If, after many floggings, he or she still cannot behave properly, then they should expel their son or have their daughter-in-law divorced . . . Even if the son likes his wife very much, if his parents are displeased with her, he should divorce her. On the other hand, if the son dislikes his wife, yet his parents say she is good at serving them, then the son should fulfill his duty as husband for the rest of his life."

DEATH RITES

The death of a family member set in motion elaborate and long-lasting ceremonies. For the head of a family the period of mourning usually lasted for three years. During that time family members wore special clothing that changed according to the length of time passed since the death.

After the death of a loved one the first duty was to place rice in the mouth of the deceased. Then the body was washed and dressed and laid in a coffin. A soul seat and a soul cloth were placed next to the coffin. Food and drink were placed on the soul

News of a Death

Neo-Confucian thinker, Zhu Xi, described every detail of proper behavior in his book, *Family Rituals*. If news of a death was received while a person was away from home, "On first learning of a parent's death, one wails, then changes clothes and departs. On the road, the bereaved wails whenever grief is felt and also on catching sight of the prefectural boundary, the county boundary, the city, and the home. On entering the gate, he goes to the front of the coffin, bows twice, then changes his clothes twice, and takes up his place for wailing."

seat every day for three months. The soul cloth was the repository of the dead person's soul while his or her body remained in the house. A banner was placed in front of the house to announce the death to friends and neighbors. Mourners brought presents such as incense, tea, candles, wine, fruit, money, or silk.

After three months the body was buried. A procession accompanied the body to the cemetery, where offerings were made to the god of earth. Food, clothing, and other gifts were buried with the body. The name of the deceased was added to the wooden tablets listing the family ancestors. During the three-year period of mourning sacrifices were made—two for good fortune and the final one for peace. If the deceased was the head of a family the ancestral tablets were changed. He was now the first generation of ancestors and the former generations were adjusted upward. Only five generations were actively venerated, and thus the newly deceased person's great-great-grandfather's tablet was "retired."

Duty to parents did not cease with their death. At least once a day someone in the family had to visit the offering hall where

Family and friends gathered at a funeral ceremony on the plain outside the city of Xi'an in Shaanxi Province, China. The family are performing the rituals and offerings necessary to ensure that the spirit of the departed is at peace.

the ancestral tablets were kept. The eldest son, as head of the family, performed regular devotions to his father and the other ancestors. Those included reports on such events as births, coming of age, and weddings. If the son had to leave on a trip lasting more than 10 days, he had to report the reasons for his upcoming absence to ancestors before departure.

Special offerings to ancestors were performed at each season of the year and on holidays. The day before a ceremony the offering hall was purified with incense; and in the hall a table was set for dinner, complete with utensils, cups, bowls, and plates. On the day itself the family rose at dawn and set out the food and drink. Then the wooden ancestral tablets were set at their places around the table. The family greeted the spirits. Then, according to Zhu Xi's book, "The spirits are urged to eat, then the door is closed. After the door is opened the sacrificed meat is taken away. Then the spirits are bid farewell . . . The leftovers are eaten."

Court Awards

A son might have the pleasure of reporting a posthumous title or promotion granted his ancestor by the court. These were often rewards that accompanied promotions won by the living. Neo-Confucian Zhu Xi's word-for-word formula for such an announcement in his *Family Rituals* reads as follows: "On such day of such month we received an edict conferring on our [name of relative] the [name of office] . . . [Name of living head of family], due to the instruction he received from his ancestors, holds a position at court beyond what he deserves. Through the grace of the sovereign, this honor has been conferred. [Head of family]'s salary came too late to support his parent, which leaves him unable to choke back his tears."

CONFUCIAN STABILITY

This, then, was the world of Confucian China. For centuries the people of the world's most populous nation followed the dictates that had been set down centuries before. Although to modern eyes their way of life might be authoritarian, stultifying, and oppressive, it produced a stable society in which each person knew his or her proper place. Rebels against the system were rare, for they faced the disapproval of living and dead alike. Few religions have had such a far-reaching influence on the daily life of so many people as Confucianism.

CHAPTER 7

A CRISIS FOR CONFUCIANISM

In the 16th and 17th centuries, great advances, developments, and changes were taking place in Europe. These included overseas exploration and establishment of trading links with the Americas, scientific and religious revolutions, and transformations in art and architecture. There were no such major changes in China. The following poem was written by Kong Shangren, a 17th-century descendant of Confucius, to express his enthusiasm about the new invention from Europe—"across the Western Seas." Eyeglasses were one of the products of the scientific revolution then beginning in Europe. Kong's reaction was typical of China's initial response to encountering European voyages of exploration.

> *White glass from across the Western Seas*
> *Is imported through Macao:*
> *Fashioned into lenses as big as coins,*
> *They encompass the eyes in a double frame.*
> *I put them on—it suddenly becomes clear;*
> *I can see the very tips of things!*
> *And read the fine print by the dim-lit window*
> *Just like in my youth.*

(In Jonathan Spence, *The Search for Modern China*.)

Painting depicting the clash between the Chinese and Japanese navies in 1894 at the Battle of the Yalu River, close to the border between China and Korea, during the first Sino-Japanese War.

Ships used to illustrate a sailing route on a historical nautical chart. Portuguese ships arrived off the southeast coast of China in 1516. The Chinese, repelled by the rough sailors with their crude ways, labeled them barbarians or foreign devils. Still, they allowed the Portuguese to use Macao on the South China Sea, south of Canton, as a trading port.

However, despite interest in and acqustion of some aspects of Western science and technology, the Chinese did not seize the opportunity to learn from Europe. In part this indifference was due to the very stability that the Confucian system provided. The Chinese officials, steeped in Confucianism, were tied to the worldview of China as the Middle Kingdom, the self-contained center of the world. In their view all essential knowledge flowed outward from China, not the other way around. This failure to adapt would be costly. Three and a half centuries after the first European vessels reached China, the Confucian worldview would be abruptly shattered.

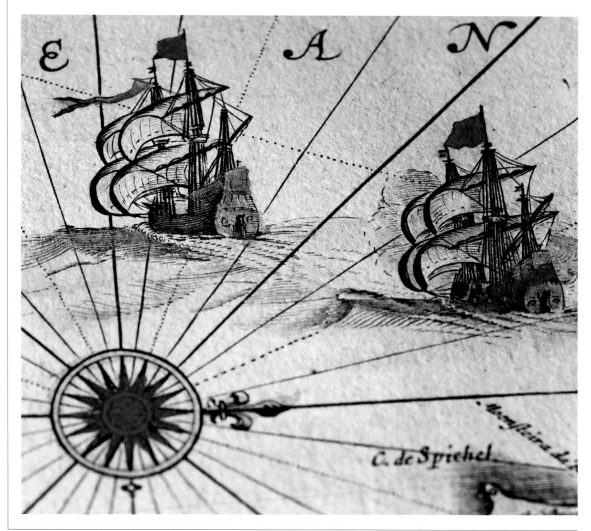

THE ARRIVAL OF THE EUROPEANS

After the arrival of the first Portuguese ships in 1516 and the establishment of Macao as a Portuguese trading post on the southeastern coast of China in 1557, other Europeans came to trade, and with the traders came missionaries determined to spread Christianity to China and other parts of the Far East.

In China the most established missionaries were the Jesuits—members of the Society of Jesus, a new Roman Catholic religious order that showed particular zeal in spreading Catholicism to Asia. Rather than trying to impose Christianity as a foreign religion and demanding that converts adopt new customs, however, the Jesuits worked to change China from within. The Jesuits learned the language and the literature of China, adopted Chinese manners, customs, and traditions, and studied the ethics and teachings of Confucianism. Their knowledge of Chinese culture enabled the Jesuits to cultivate friendships with educated Chinese officials. In 1601 Matteo Ricci, a Jesuit priest, was permitted to come to the capital, Beijing, and set up a missionary headquarters.

EUROPEAN INFLUENCES

With their deep scientific knowledge and respect for Chinese culture, the Jesuits made a favorable impression. Chinese officials were fascinated by such inventions as European clocks. The Jesuits' skills in mathematics, calendar making, and geography earned them favor in the imperial court. Jesuit priest Matteo Ricci displayed a map of the world—with Europe in the center. It offended the Chinese, so Ricci prepared a new map with China in the center. That map was more favorably received.

CHRISTIANITY IN A CHINESE CONTEXT

At the same time the Jesuits were explaining Christianity to the members of the court and the mandarins. They used terms familiar to the Chinese. For example, they equated the Chinese term for heaven, *tien,* with the Christian God. They showed marked respect for Confucius and his teachings. The Jesuits accepted ancestor worship, believing that it was an expression of respect rather than a religious practice. They regarded some of the popular rituals honoring Confucius as signs of respect for the sage's teachings, which the Jesuits felt did not conflict with Christianity.

The Jesuits' tolerant approach initially met with some success at the Chinese court. The Chinese were willing to accept Christian beliefs because in their philosophy, one religion did not negate the truth of another. Jesuits began to make Catholic converts in the closed circle of the court. By the 1640s, Chinese Catholicism could claim not only many members of the court but also the heir to the throne.

Buddhism, Confucianism, Daoism—All as One

Matteo Ricci, the Jesuit priest who lived in China from 1583 to 1610, reported that many Confucians also followed Buddhism or Daoism. He wrote: "The commonest opinion held here among those who consider themselves the most wise is to say that all three of these sects come together as one, and that you can hold them all at once . . . (such people feel) that as far as religion is concerned the more ways of talking about religion there are, all the more benefit will that bring to the kingdom." However, he felt that "in this (opinion) they deceive themselves and others and lead to great disorder."

(In Jonathan Spence, *The Memory Palace of Matteo Ricci.*)

The Great Wall of China has a 2,000-year history although many of the sections visible today date from the Ming dynasty. The wall stretches from the east of China to its west and is more than 4,000 miles (6,400 kilometers) long, although parts of it are in ruins or have disappeared.

In 1644 the 276-year-old Ming dynasty faced invaders from the north—the Manchus, who lived in the northeast beyond the Great Wall, the 1,450-mile (2,250-kilometer)-long defensive wall built from 214 B.C.E. to repel Turkish and Mongol invaders. The Manchus captured the imperial capital and established the Qing dynasty. Although the Jesuits had supported and aided the Ming forces, the new Qing rulers permitted them to remain.

However now the Jesuits' attempts to bring Christianity to China were being hampered by other Catholic European religious orders who were appalled at the Jesuits' willingness to accept so many Confucian practices and beliefs. The Dominicans and the Franciscans demanded that the Chinese accept Christianity exclusively. They accused the Jesuits of distorting Christianity.

DECLINE OF CHINESE CHRISTIANITY

The idea that there was only one true faith did not harmonize with the Chinese view of religion, however. The argument was presented to the pope. After a debate that went on for over a century, the pope ruled against the Jesuits. Christianity made no further headway in China.

While the Chinese were getting a glimpse of the West the missionaries were writing home about China. Matteo Ricci translated the Chinese Classics, making some of the richness of the Chinese heritage available in Europe. In the 18th century, a time of intellectual ferment in Europe, such important figures as François-Marie Arouet (more popularly known as Voltaire), Gottfried Wilhelm von Leibniz, and Denis Diderot were impressed by Confucius's teachings. They saw Chinese civilization as humanistic and rational, not torn by religious fanaticism as the Europe of their time was. For a brief time some teachers and philosophers even proposed Confucius as a model for Europe. This early contact between the West and China gave the Chinese a chance to see the achievements of a different culture. It offered the Chinese the stimulation of new ideas and inventions. However few Chinese knew of or were influenced by Western thought. Change seemed unnecessary because most Chinese were very content with their civilization and with Confucianism.

QING CONFUCIANISM

Before the Manchus conquered China they had a kingdom in Manchuria, in China's northeastern region. Over time they had come into contact with Chinese civilization and had adopted many of its ideas. Confucian ceremony was already a part of the-

Manchu kingdom. When they came to power the Manchus soon became more Confucian than the Chinese. The Qing emperors continued to perform the age-old rituals to heaven and strongly endorsed Confucian studies.

THE KANGXI EMPEROR

The greatest member of the Qing dynasty, the Kangxi emperor (r. 1662–1722), strove to be a model Confucian ruler. The emperor began each day by listening to a lecture on the Confucian Classics, and he is said to have constantly reminded himself that one act of negligence on his part "may cause sorrow all through the country." He practiced what he preached, making great efforts to control flooding, personally visiting distant parts of his realm, and reducing taxes many times during his long reign. He was a great patron of learning and art, sponsoring the writing of a dictionary as well as an encyclopedia that ran to more than 5,000 volumes.

NATIONAL CONFIDENCE AND PRIDE

During the 17th and 18th centuries both the Manchu rulers and the Chinese were confident that theirs was the greatest civilization in the world. Their Confucian state was grounded in religion. The state rites provided grandeur and acted out the philosophy of the universe espoused by the Neo-Confucians. While heaven controlled destiny, earth provided nourishment. Heaven, earth, and humanity formed a trinity. The highest function of the emperor, who owed his appointment to heaven, was to make sure through his personal virtue and action that human affairs were conducted according to the will of heaven. He had to make sure that the nourishing power of earth was used

The Sacred Edict of 16 Articles

In 1672 the Kangxi emperor (r. 1662–1722), who strove to be a model Confucian ruler, promulgated the Sacred Edict of 16 Articles. These were maxims summarizing Confucian principles in simple language. The first, for example, exhorted the people to "pay just regard to filial and fraternal duties." Through the 16 Articles the emperor aimed to bring harmony to his realm by spreading Confucian values. The Articles were read in the schools and public squares on the first and 15th days of each lunar month—a practice that continued in villages and towns until the 20th century.

Confucian Values

All over China homes held statues of gods arranged in a hierarchical order that reflected the Confucian order of importance. Nor could Daoism and Buddhism resist its influence. Their elaborate systems of many heavens and hells came to be ranked much like an extensive Confucian government. Confucian values were even found in a popular board game, the goal of which was to become an official.

for the good of his subjects. When all worked correctly the whole universe was in harmony. Although the population did not take part in these rites, the concepts of Confucianism filtered downward.

Temples—which were often also schools—to Confucius were found in every town of the empire. The temple-schools taught Confucian doctrine, and under the sponsorship of the Qing rulers more temple-schools were established so that most of the villages had at least one. On the first day of school the young Chinese scholar paid homage to Confucius, ensuring that Confucius would always be uppermost in his thoughts. Twice a month the imperial Sacred Edict of 16 Articles, the maxims summarizing Confucian principles in simple language, was read aloud. Students learned the Five Classics by heart and thought of Confucius as the man who had molded their civilization.

Confucianism influenced society at all levels. Each family followed the practices of ancestor worship. Even the popular deities in Daoism and Buddhism that were not part of Confucianism reflected its influence.

DECLINE WITHIN CHINA

The very success of Confucianism bred conservatism and resistance to change. Although Confucius had looked to the past for guidance, he was open to new ideas. However now, by the end of the 18th century, Confucianism was still set in the traditional ways of the past. The imperial examinations followed the strict form that had been instituted during the Ming dynasty. A successful student had not only to demonstrate knowledge of the Zhu Xi form of Confucianism but also to write it in the proper form, the "eight-legged essay." Candidates bought preparatory books much like the College Board study books of today. They had to memorize the enormous literature of traditional Confucianism; creativity in writing the answers guaranteed failure. The original thoughts of Confucius were becoming lost in rote memorization. His ideas were becoming a formula. By limiting the intellectual talent of the nation with this narrow formula, China started to stagnate.

THE SHOCK OF DEFEAT

In the 19th century the European nations and the United States became more aggressive in trying to establish a regular trading relationship with China. The Chinese government restricted all foreign traders to the area around the port of Canton. The emperor refused to allow foreign governments to establish regular diplomatic relations with his court. The Confucian world order did not allow equal relationships with those they regarded as inferior.

OPIUM AND ITS SPREAD

However, as China stagnated, Western nations moved forward with scientific and industrial revolutions. Now Europeans and Americans were engaged in a race to develop markets for their products. Previously China had been self-sufficient and had little use for foreign goods. However the British hit on a product that had wide appeal: opium. After British ships began to bring opium from their colony in India, China became flooded with the drug and a serious addiction problem developed.

The Road to Success

The Confucian system was self-regulating. Through the examination system it provided the "priests" of Confucianism. The examination system was the single road to success in China. No merchant, no matter how wealthy, was as respected as a government official. Every family hoped that one of its sons would have enough ability to pass the exams. Those who passed the exams had a strong incentive to support and continue the system. And during the Qing dynasty (1644–1911) Neo-Confucianism provided a stability and a prosperity that seemed stable and permanent.

Yet this high point marked the beginning of a decline. Scholars who carefully read the *Yi Jing*, one of the Five Classics, might have seen this. The name of the 55th hexagram of the book is *feng*, meaning "abundance" or "fullness."

The text describes it:
Abundance has success.
The king attains abundance.
Be not sad.
Be like the sun at midday.

However as one of the appendices to the *Yi Jing* points out:
"When the sun stands at midday, it begins to set."

The emperor responded by forbidding the use or the importing of opium. However by then its use was already widespread, and it continued to be smuggled through Canton. In 1839 the emperor appointed one of his most respected officials, Lin Zexu, as a special commissioner. Lin's assignment was to go to Canton and clear up the problem.

Commissioner Lin wrote Queen Victoria of Great Britain a now-famous letter asking her to stop the opium trade. Calling on her better nature he reminded her that she would not want the effects of drug abuse for her own subjects. Thus, Lin asked, why did she allow her merchants to sell it to others? It is not known whether Victoria received the letter, but there was no reply to his appeal.

Commissioner Lin was the premier product of the Confucian system, and he attacked the problem in a typical Confucian way. In public proclamations he told of the evil effects of the drugs. He ordered all smokers to turn over their opium and drug paraphernalia. He called 600 students to a special session. After asking them conventional questions about the Chinese Classics, he asked them to name the drug dealers they knew and what they would do about the drug problem. It was an interesting twist on the examination system.

Lin felt that an appeal to reason and virtue would sway the British ruler, Queen Victoria, but he received no response from her. So the imperial commissioner took the dramatic step of taking the foreign merchants prisoner, holding them hostage until they agreed to surrender the opium in their ships. They complied. After offering a sacrifice in apology to the spirit of the southern sea, Lin dumped the cargoes of opium into the ocean.

This action brought on the Opium War (1839–42) between China and Great Britain. It was a one-sided conflict. British warships sank the smaller, lightly armed Chinese ships and took control of the coast. When British troops landed and marched toward Beijing, the emperor asked for peace terms.

FOREIGN SETTLEMENT IN CHINA

The Chinese defeat brought about a revolution in China's relationships with foreign countries. More ports were opened to foreign trade, and the island of Hong Kong was ceded to Britain. Other European powers demanded equal treatment. China was forced to allow the foreigners to live in its cities, giving them extraterritoriality. This meant that foreigners accused of crimes were tried in their own courts, even if the victims of the crime were Chinese. Extraterritoriality showed the foreigners' open contempt for the legal system of China.

Yet the Chinese were powerless to resist. Other military defeats brought more loss of territory. In a war with France in 1884 China lost its big brother/little brother relationship with Vietnam. France moved to make Vietnam and the rest of Southeast Asia a colony. In treaties with Western nations, China lost control over its tariffs on foreign goods. Christian missionaries were free to roam the country to try to make converts.

This series of defeats was a profound shock to China and the Confucian system. The emperor's scholar-officials asked themselves this question: How could China be so weak in relation to the Western countries? It was a question that Chinese officials tried to come to grips with for the next 100 years. During that time China struggled with the problem of how to remain true to the Confucian tradition while adapting to the wider world that had so rudely thrust itself into China's affairs.

The Chinese government's initial reaction to its humiliation was to call for a strengthening of traditional values. Many scholars felt that China's weakness was the result of not holding closely enough to Confucian traditions. Others, such as Commissioner Lin himself, realized that the Chinese needed to learn more about the West and its scientific and technological skills. A prince of the imperial family sought to modernize China's military forces by adopting Western technology, training, and procurement of equipment. Scholars set to work translating foreign works of geography, history, politics, and law. This phase was known as the Self-Strengthening Movement.

DEFEAT BY JAPAN

Yet change came slowly to Chinese society, with its centuries of adherence to the Confucian ways. China's smaller neighbor, Japan, proved more adaptable. Using Western advisors, Japan built its own military force and invaded Korea in 1894. Korea turned to China for help.

The resulting conflict was the greatest of China's humiliations. The Japanese fleet soundly defeated the Chinese ships, and Japanese troops landed on Chinese soil. In the peace negotiations China was forced to cede some of its territory to Japan. The Confucian world order was turned upside down. Japan, which had learned Confucianism from China, defeated the nation that had long regarded itself as the teacher and parent of Asia.

THE LAST GREAT CONFUCIAN

The shock of this defeat galvanized some of China's younger scholars into action. In the spring of 1895, gathering at the *jin-shi* (highest grade) examinations in Beijing, these young men found others of the same mind. They presented a long "memorial," or proposal, to the imperial court, setting forth a program of modernization and reform. The leader of this group was Kang Youwei, a 37-year-old scholar from the Canton area. Kang had already attracted attention for his command of the Confucian Classics and his unusual interpretations of them. He had argued that Confucius had not resisted social change and that Confucianism should not be a bar to development and progress. It may have been this very creativity that had prevented Kang from passing the highest level of the examination system.

RENEWING THE OLD, ACCEPTING THE NEW

Kang had carefully studied Western scientific works and was also influenced by Buddhism. His goal became to create a synthesis of old and new, preserving the essence of Confucianism while taking what was appropriate from other traditions. He saw himself as a new sage determined to overthrow the stultifying system. He strongly criticized Neo-Confucianism, claiming that it had distorted Confucius's original teachings. For the rest of his life he would seek to save Confucianism by renewing it in his own fashion.

The young scholars' proposal found a sympathetic ear in the emperor Guangxu, who had studied English and was eager to modernize his reign. However the emperor was only 24 and still dominated by his elderly aunt, Cixi, known as the dowager empress. Three years later, however, with his aunt in retirement at her lavish summer palace, Guangxu acted on the proposal. He issued a series of decrees aimed at modernizing China.

Kang Youwei and other reform-minded scholars were appointed as secretaries in the emperor's council. The entrenched Neo-Confucian bureaucracy saw Guangxu's decrees as a threat to their power, however. Many sincerely felt that overturning the

大清國當今慈禧端佑康頤昭豫莊誠壽恭欽獻崇熙皇太后聖母皇

Portrait of Cixi, the "dowager empress" of China, whose stubborn resistance to change within China led to a revolution that overthrew the last Chinese emperor and caused his official abdication as the Son of Heaven in 1912.

Neo-Confucian system would strip China of its core values. Abruptly, in September 1898 the dowager empress returned to the capital and seized control of the government. She announced that the emperor had asked her to resume power. In reality he was imprisoned on an island in the palace grounds. The dowager empress executed several of his young advisers. Fortunately for Kang Youwei he had left the city a short time before. He escaped to Hong Kong, later returned to China, and then left for Canada.

THE BOXER REBELLION

The Qing dynasty had lost its last opportunity to save itself by reforming the Confucian system. Two years later, in 1900, with the encouragement of government officials, a secret society whose members were called Boxers attacked Westerners living in China and began to destroy everything and anyone involved in the Western culture in China. The Boxer Rebellion, as it is known, burned missionary churches, houses in the foreign sections of Chinese cities, and diplomatic embassies. Finally an eight-nation military force invaded China and ended the rebellion. This action ended China's illusions about its supremacy.

Too late the dowager empress saw the need for reform. At her invitation some officials presented another proposal to the throne. It concluded, "Unless we cultivate talents, we cannot expect to exist. Unless we promote education we cannot cultivate talents. Unless we reform civil and military examinations, we cannot promote education." The empress responded by abolishing the examination system, setting up modern schools, and sending Chinese students to study abroad.

The Hundred Days Reform

The "Hundred Days Reform" called for the overhaul of the examination system. The eight-legged essay would be dropped, along with tests on fine calligraphy and poetry. Instead questions would focus on practical governmental problems. Indeed, the entire Chinese school system would now prepare students not to be Confucian scholars but experts in such subjects as mining, medicine, agriculture, and the development of industry. Guangxu also made sweeping changes in the government structure, establishing bureaus to deal with foreign trade, the production of export goods, mines, railways, and a government budget. The reforms addressed China's military needs with a plan to build or purchase modern warships that would be the equal of any nation's.

義和童子軍

後隊大砲兵

埋伏國

A print depicting English and French troops during the Boxer Rebellion of 1900. When foreign soldiers crushed the rebellion, China's rulers realized—too late—that changes were needed in the ancient Confucian examination system and in the country's constitutional structure.

THE LAST EMPEROR

Chinese scholars had studied Western forms of government to learn the secret of the West's success. They found that the governments of most of the Western nations were controlled by elected officials. Japan too had overthrown the Tokugawa shogunate and adopted a constitutional form of government with an elected legislature—though the Japanese emperor continued to rule officially. Guided by these examples various movements

圖戰鏖民團與軍陸法英

sprang up to bring constitutional government to China. In 1911 revolution broke out, and on February 12, 1912, the last dynasty in China's long history fell. With the abdication of the last Son of Heaven no one was left to carry out the ancient Confucian rites for the nation. As China faced a new and uncertain future one of the most important questions was what role Confucianism would have in it.

CHAPTER 8

CONFUCIANISM INTO THE TWENTY–FIRST CENTURY

As China moved from ancient empire to modern and fragile republic, Confucianism's survival was hardly guaranteed. Many argued that it was a dead tradition, lacking the innovative spirit needed to transform China into a modern nation. Circumstances seemed to support this opinion. From the perspective of the ancient Celestial Empire the Chinese world was horribly disfigured: Vietnam was now a French colony, Korea had been annexed by Japan, and the Japanese were now looking toward Europe rather than China.

History has shown that rumors of Confucianism's demise were greatly exaggerated. China and other nations of the Confucian world have been wracked by war and revolution. Yet despite this Confucianism has survived. Now into a new century, the future of Confucianism is unclear, but there are positive signs that Confucianism is once again adapting to new circumstanc-

A performance staged to mark the 2,557th anniversary of the birth of Confucius. The ceremony took place on September 28, 2006 in the Confucian Temple, at Qufu in Shandong Province.

es and offering its wisdom to new generations in east Asia and beyond. With the new openness of the Chinese government to Confucianism, that influence will likely increase.

CONFUCIANISM DURING THE REPUBLIC

In the period between the dowager empress, Cixi, who dominated the young emperor Guangxu (r. 1875–1908), and the birth of the republic in 1912, more radical pro-Western notions had gained popularity. Many leading voices were all too willing to rid China of any vestiges of Confucius. However there were political leaders in the new republic who believed that Confucianism could support this novel form of government. Sun Yat-sen, the first president, declared that "Confucius and Mencius were both exponents of democracy." Not all agreed. Yuan Shih-kai, a former imperial general, succeeded Sun Yat-sen as president. Under his leadership a serious attempt was made to reinstate the sacrificial rites. As president he continued the spring and autumn rituals at the Confucian temple in Beijing. Yuan ordered local government officials to continue ceremonies at the Confucian temples throughout China.

WARLORDS AND YOUNG LEADERS

Yuan Shih-kai's viewpoints reflected elements of the new conservative movement's basic program: the study of the Confucian classics and restoration of Confucianism to its central place in China. Unfortunately for the conservatives Yuan proved to be a disastrous leader, for during his four years as president he slowly increased his authority with the hope of restoring a monarchy. Ultimately his plan failed, and his self-serving imperial drive led the country into lawlessness and disorder upon his death in 1916. Though the republican government continued to exist, warlords with their own armies controlled large areas of the country. Yuan's misadventure increased anti-Confucianism among China's Western-trained youth, who were now convinced that unless China discarded the old system social and political progress were impossible.

One of the most influential of the young leaders was Chen Duxiu (1879–1942), a popular French-trained professor at Beijing University. Through his magazine *New Youth* he called on China's young generation to renew the country and to do away with things of the past. He argued for Westernization and the adoption of science and democracy. He urged his readers "to fight Confucianism, the old tradition of virtue and rituals, the old ethics and the old politics, the old learning and the old literature."

The May Fourth Movement of 1919 was due largely to the increasing influence of people like Chen Duxiu. On that day 5,000 students took to Beijing's streets to protest the Treaty of Versailles, the peace settlement ending World War I (1914–18). The Versailles Treaty granted Japan rights to the province of Shantung, the ancestral home of Confucius. The Chinese viewed this as a serious betrayal, since they had joined the Western allies in the war. The accession to Japan reinforced Chinese fears about their weak country and the necessity of Chinese self-reliance. Demonstrations spread throughout China. In many cities Confucianism was targeted. Even in Qufu, the home of Confucius, students paraded and chanted the slogan, "Destroy the old curiosity shop of Confucianism." This cry became a national slogan for the rejection of traditional culture.

CHIANG KAI-SHEK

By the late 1920s the health of the republic had improved but concerns about Confucianism's place in Chinese culture persisted. General Chiang Kai-shek, the ideological successor to Sun Yat-sen, defeated the warlords, thus unifying most of the country. Confucianism made a small but significant comeback under his leadership. Chiang ordered his military officers to dedicate their free time to reading the Confucian classics, he made Confucius's

Japanese Rule in China

From 1937 to 1945 the Chinese suffered under brutal Japanese occupation. Ironically the Japanese treated Confucian temples with more respect than they did the Chinese people. At the Confucian Temple at Qufu, the home of Confucius, for example, the Japanese continued to offer temple sacrifices throughout the occupation. Remarkably biscuits left by the fleeing Kong family at the time of Japanese invasion were found undisturbed after the war.

birthday a national holiday, and his government provided protection for Confucian temples. In 1934 Chiang inaugurated the New Life Movement based on the Confucian virtues. However it would be short-lived.

CONFUCIANISM UNDER COMMUNISM

After World War II (1939–45) China was seized by a violent civil war between Chiang Kai-shek's national government and Communist rebels led by Mao Zedong. In 1949 the Communists emerged victorious, establishing the People's Republic of China. The Communist government had little tolerance for religion, the "opiate of the people," being unscientific and thus obsolete. "I hated Confucius from the age of eight," Mao told his followers. According to the Chairman, Confucianism helped a small group of people amass power for themselves at the majority's expense.

The irony of Mao's rejection of Confucianism is that he exhibited many traditional Chinese characteristics. Both Chinese and

China's national flag was adopted in 1949 at the founding of the People's Republic of China. The large star symbolizes the Communist Party and the small stars represent the people of China.

Western observers note that he ruled China in much the same way as the emperors he criticized.

Marxist ideology as interpreted by Mao became the basis for a new system of ethics as pervasive as Confucian ethics had been. Marxism, named after its founder German philosopher and economist Karl Marx (1818–83), supposes that through conflict the succession of feudalism, capitalism, socialism, and a classless society is inevitable. Communist cells and study groups replaced the family as the enforcers of social stability. Even Mao's special brand of Marxism exhibited a classical Chinese worldview. Breaking from the communism of Russia, he understood China as teacher of the nations and sought to spread his own form of Marxism throughout the world. Arguably much of this would not have been possible without China's deep Confucian roots.

Statue in China of Mao Zedong who led the Communist rebels to victory in 1949. Although Mao rejected the Five Classics, he understood the importance of literature and the written word. Mao's *Red Book*, filled with his own revolutionary Communist maxims, replaced the *Five Classics*.

THE CULTURAL REVOLUTION

The greatest damage to Confucianism came during the turmoil of the Cultural Revolution, a decade-long campaign designed by Mao to reinstill the revolutionary fervor of the past, to destabilize the then-entrenched Chinese Communist Party, and finally to root out traditional Chinese culture.

Ardent young Maoists called Red Guards went on a nationwide rampage, destroying lives and national cultural treasures. Confucian tombs in the forest of Qufu were vandalized; temples were either destroyed or turned into factories; schools were closed; teachers were humiliated publicly, often killed, or sent away to work on farms. In 1974 Mao ordered an intensification of the fight against Confucius. Persecution subsided only after Mao's death two years later.

THE AFTERMATH

Since 1976 government repression of religion has relaxed considerably. In 1979 the state changed its official policy, asserting religion's role in "the development of human society." The result has been a Chinese religious renaissance. Though still officially atheist, the Communist government continues to show signs of gradual openness in the economic, political, and religious spheres of life. The government still holds a firm grip on religious practice, however. Ever fearful of religion's threatening influence on society and the government, it represses "unofficial" groups deemed potentially subversive and unpatriotic.

While Buddhism and Daoism revived immediately after the end of the Cultural Revolution, the Confucian temples long remained empty monuments to a past age. In recent years, though, worshippers have returned—not in the droves that visit Buddhist temples or climb Daoist sacred mountains, but enough to give the few remaining Confucian temples a sense of life returning. However very few Confucian temples are still in existence, compared with the thousands of Buddhist and Daoist temples. And the few that remain are only really busy at examination times when students visit to make offerings for successful results.

NEW CONFUCIAN TEACHINGS

Although New Confucians represent a diverse group some generalizations can be made about their basic teachings. Central to New Confucianism is the stress on reviving two traditional Confucian themes: the unification of inner virtue (*neishing*, "sageliness within") with external merits (*waiwang*, "kingliness without"), and the unification of the natural and moral orders. Another characteristic is the movement's cosmopolitanism. New Confucians seek to balance the insights of the West with the teachings of Confucianism. While often critical of the Occident, they are generally open to Western art, science, and technology inasmuch as these support Confucian norms. Gone are the days of Confucian self-congratulation and fearful isolation. Finally the movement may also be identified by its belief that Confucianism is fundamentally an inclusive humanism. The virtue of *ren*, or humanity, is the true mark of genuine Confucianism, and it may not be isolated to Chinese culture alone. *Ren* lies at the heart of all social ethics, personal cultivation, and thought.

LIVING CONFUCIANISM

It might appear that the early-20th-century debate on China's future was divided between only two forces: conservatives who hoped to restore Confucianism and radicals who believed in total Westernization. However there were others who adopted a more constructive attitude. "New Confucians" are dedicated to reform and reclamation of the value and spirit of Confucianism for the modern world. Over the last hundred years they have been outspoken critics of the tradition and of reformist thought within their own movement. Though called New Confucians they understand their project as being in continuity with the early Confucian tradition.

In the years following the Maoist takeover of China formal renewal of Confucianism declined in the land of its birth. Confucian thought shifted to Hong Kong, Taiwan, and the United States. In this new period New Confucians were not just writing books, but also founding and revitalizing Confucian educational institutions. New Asia College, Hong Kong, is one example. The college embodies the New Confucian endeavor. Its goal is to revitalize the spirit of learning that once characterized the Song and Ming Dynasties. Reflecting the movement's basic openness, it

A procession of traditionally dressed Confucian students, officials, and teachers celebrating the birthday of Confucius in the town of Qufu. Birthday celebrations are traditionally held for Confucius on September 28th not only in China, but also in Taiwan and Korea.

SOUTH KOREA

South Korea, one of China's "little brothers," continues its Confucian ways. Like Taiwan, it celebrates Confucius's birthday (September 28). Seoul's Sung Kyun University, founded in 1398 by King Taejo of the Chosun dynasty, is the oldest university in Korea. While the curriculum has expanded, the institution maintains its original purpose: to enlighten the people of Korea and to produce national leaders in government and scholarship based on Confucian philosophy and ethics. The ancient spring and autumn rituals are still performed at Seoul's major Confucian shrine. Dancers and musicians play as scarlet-robed Confucian scholar-officials perform the same steps that were used during the Yi dynasty (1392–1910).

borrows the tutorial system of European universities, directs students in the studies of the humanities, and serves as a bridge between East and West.

HONORING CONFUCIUS

Throughout the Chinese-speaking world, one can still observe Confucian rituals and ceremonies. In Hong Kong Confucius's birthday (September 28) is commemorated at the city's temple. In Taiwan, where the 77th descendant of Confucius lives today, Confucius' birthday is known as Teacher's Day. During this national holiday all teachers are honored for continuing the great tradition of the "Teacher of All Generations." Special services, including dances dating from the Ming dynasty, are conducted at the Confucian temples on the island. And in June throughout the Chinese world, the Dragon Boat Festival commemorates the death in 299 B.C.E. of the Confucian statesman Chu Yuan, who drowned himself to call attention to the need for government reform. Reform, remember, is not new to Confucianism but has been part of the tradition from the beginning.

ECONOMIC GROWTH THROUGHOUT ASIA

Confucianism suffered for much of the 20th century because of its identification with China's imperial past. By the 1970s economic changes in east Asia forced critics to look anew at the region. Japanese technology began to flood Western markets, transforming the country into the world's second-largest economy. By the 1980s Japan had been joined by Singapore, South Korea, Taiwan, and Hong Kong as some of the most vital national economies. Economic liberalization in the People's Republic, begun in 1979 with political reforms, continues to transform China. Since the reforms began the economy has grown annually by an impressive amount. The promise of an economically viable China has attracted more than $400 billion from overseas investors since 1979. The global recession of 2008 has slowed but not stopped this surge.

China's economic transformation has granted it increased international influence. The United States once thought of China as a helpful counter to the old Soviet Union, but now recognizes it as a major competitor, leading the rest of the region into what may become known as the "Asian century." By the late 1990s, it was evident that east Asia could no longer be considered a backward relic of a more glorious past. And ironically the religion once blamed for all the woes of the Orient has in recent years been credited with fueling its economic success. While an overstatement and too often used without any real understanding of Confucianism, it nevertheless has a kernel of truth. Hard work, respect for authority, familial stability, the importance of education, and concern for the common good are Confucian values now identified with the successful Asian transition into the modern world. Many Westerners now look to Asia for new models of modernization and industrialization.

CONFUCIANISM IN THE WEST

Confucianism has been an international movement for centuries, shaping the cultures of Korea, Vietnam, and Japan, and thus fashioning the so-called "Confucian world." In the 20th century, with increasing immigration and globalization, Confucianism's scope increased beyond east Asia. Confucianism is no longer merely an Asian phenomenon, but an international one. Not everyone believes that Confu-

BOSTON CONFUCIANISM

The name of a new, experimental school of Confucian thought and practice is "Boston Confucianism." The name refers not only to scholars located in Boston, Massachusetts, but to those in the West and Asia who believe that Confucianism has achieved the status of a world philosophy. Just as American philosophers without Greek ancestry often subscribe to the teachings of Plato or Aristotle, Boston Confucians argue that a Westerner—or African or Indian—may subscribe to the teachings of the Confucian tradition. Moreover they believe that Confucianism has the tools to enrich Western culture and that Western culture has something of value to offer Confucianism. Both East and West stand to benefit from the encounter, they argue.

cianism can be successfully transplanted from its east Asian context, or that one can be a Western Confucian, but many do.

CONFUCIANISM INTO THE FUTURE

What might the future hold for Confucianism? The answer to such a question is really impossible to determine, but we can get a sense of the future by examining what is taking place in Confucianism today. As we have seen, the Chinese government is loosening its restrictions on religion. Around east Asia scholarly institutions are thriving, and temples are either being restored or are continuing to serve the faithful. The Chinese government is opening "Confucius Centers" around the world where anyone can come and learn about China past and present. Far from rejecting the values of Confucius, modern China appears to want to emulate them.

Jongmayo Shrine in Seoul is the oldest preserved Confucian royal shrine in South Korea. The shrine has existed in its present form since the 16th century and houses tablets containing the teachings of the Choson royal dynasty (1392–1910). Confucian rites, including ritual music and dance, continue to be performed in the Jongmayo Shrine.

New Confucians, the leaders in the restoration, admit that Confucianism has done a much better job developing sageliness within than it has developing kingliness without. They understand that Confucianism's task is to articulate a modern political vision engaging the lived realities of Asians. Confucianism's contribution in the 21st century will not be the fixed social and political life of the Chinese dynasties, they argue, but the tradition's moral and spiritual values. These values, undergirded by *ren*, or humanity, include an ethic of responsibility, the importance of comprehensive education, and a humanistic understanding of life.

The year 1999 marked the 2,550th anniversary of Confucius's birth. Qufu, the Master's ancestral home, stood witness to the turbulent decades of the 20th century. Today, thankfully, the treasures of Qufu are undergoing restoration, while a new Research Institute of Confucianism stands nearby. Fusing elements of both Song dynasty and modern architecture, the new center promises to become a beacon of Confucianism in the 21st century. Perhaps Qufu is a fitting symbol of modern Confucianism: restoration and renovation of Confucian treasures coupled with new facilities skillfully combining the ancient and modern. As the new century begins Confucianism, like Qufu itself, looks out into a world of challenge and promise. Many in that world desire the same things Confucius sought: an orderly society; a balance between nature and humankind; and a way of conducting oneself with kindness, charity, honesty, and faithfulness. To people such as these, Confucius seems anything but outdated.

A statue of Confucius at Jongmayo Shrine. It stands as a visible link between the past and future of Confucianism.

FACT FILE

Worldwide Numbers
There are about 6 million people in the world who call themselves Confucianists, the followers of Confucianism.

Holy Symbol
The character for the word *li* is symbolic of Confucianism. *Li* is the correct behavior, the principles, and the essence of Confucian thinking.

Founders
The founder is Confucius, who lived from 551 to 479 B.C.E.

Holy Writings
The most important basic texts of Confucianism are the Five Classics. These are China's oldest literature and are believed to have been edited by Confucius. They comprise the *Book of Poetry, Book of Rites, Book of History, Spring and Autumn Annals,* and *Book of Changes.*

Holy Places
The main pilgrimage site is Qufu in China, the birthplace of Confucius.

Festivals
The main celebration is for Confucius's birthday (September 28). It is celebrated throughout East Asia.

BIBLIOGRAPHY

Creel, H.G. *Chinese Thought from Confucius to Mao Tse-tung.* New York: Mentor Book, 1953.

DeBary, William Theodore. *Sources of Chinese Tradition.* New York: Columbia University Press, 1999.

Ebrey, Patricia Buckley. *Chinese Civilization and Society: A Sourcebook.* New York: Free Press, 1981.

Haboush, JaHyun Kim. *A Heritage of Kings: One Man's Monarchy in the Confucian World.* Studies in Oriental culture, no. 21. New York: Columbia University Press, 1988.

Hsu, Francis L. K. *The Challenge of the American Dream: The Chinese in the United States.* Minorities in American life series. Belmont, Calif.: Wadsworth Pub. Co, 1971.

Kwok, Man-Ho, Martin Palmer, and Jay Ramsay. *Tao Te Ching: A New Translation.* Dorset, Mass.: Element, 1993.

Seeger, Elizabeth. *Eastern Religions.* New York: Crowell, 1973.

Spence, Jonathan D. *The Memory Palace of Matteo Ricci.* London: Quercus, 2008.

Spence, Jonathan D. *The Search for Modern China.* New York: Norton, 2002.

Swann, Nancy Lee. *Pan Chao, Foremost Woman Scholar of China.* Ann Arbor: Center for Chinese Studies, The University of Michigan, 2001.

Totman, Conrad D. *Japan Before Perry: A Short History.* Berkeley, Calif.: University of California Press, 2008.

Waley, Arthur (trans.). *The Book of Songs.* London: Routledge, 2005.

FURTHER READING

Berthrong, John H. *Transformations of the Confucian Way*. Boulder, Colo.: Westview Press, 1998.

Berthrong, John H., and Evelyn Nagai Berthrong. *Confucianism: A Short Introduction*. Oxford: Oneworld Publications, 2000.

Chin, Annping. *The Authentic Confucius: A Life of Thought and Politics*. New York: Scribner, 2007.

Confucius. *The Analects*. Translated by D.C. Lau. New York: Penguin Group, 1979.

Creel, H.G. *Confucius and the Chinese Way*. New York: Peter Smith Pub., 2000.

Grayson, James Huntley. *Korea: A Religious History, Revised Edition*. New York: Routledge Curzon, 2002.

Ellwood, Robert, and Gregory Alles, eds. *The Encyclopedia of World Religions*. New York: Facts On File, 1998.

Hsu, Immanuel C.Y. *The Rise of Modern China, 6th ed*. New York: Oxford University Press, 2000.

Neville, Robert Cummings. *Boston Confucianism: Portable Tradition in the Late-Modern World*. Albany: State University of New York Press, 2000.

Phillips, Richard T. *China Since 1911*. New York: St. Martin's Press, 1996.

Schirokauer, Conrad. *A Brief History of Chinese and Japanese Civilizations*. Stamford, Conn.: International Thomson Publishing, 1994.

Yao, Xinzhong. *An Introduction to Confucianism*. Cambridge: Cambridge University Press, 2000.

Zhu, Xi and Patricia Buckley Ebrey. *Chu Hsi's Family Rituals: A Twelfth-Century Chinese Manual for the Performance of Cappings, Weddings, Funerals, and Ancestral Rites*. Princeton, N.J.: Princeton University Press, 1991.

WEB SITES

Further facts and figures, history, and current status of the religion can be found on the following Web sites:

plato.stanford.edu/entries/confucius/
Stanford Encyclopedia of Philosophy entry on the life and teachings of Confucius.

www.brainyquote.com/quotes/authors/c/ confucius.html
This Web site page lists many quotes of Confucius.

www.crystalinks.com/confucianism.html
An illustrated article reviewing the basic Confucian teachings and the history of Confucianism.

www.religioustolerance.org/confuciu.htm
This site provides a summary of all major religions, including Confucianism, and acts as a portal to other sites about Confucius and his beliefs and sayings.

GLOSSARY

Analects—A collection of Confucius's conversations and pronouncements on the proper conduct of life, which, according to Chinese tradition, were recorded by his disciples soon after his death.

ancestor worship—In China, reverence toward one's ancestors. In Confucianism, an aspect of filial devotion that consists of rituals carried out by the head of the household to honor deceased family members.

Buddhism—A religion that came from India to China (in the first century C.E.), where it was influenced by Confucianism and Daoism and became one of the three great faiths. Mahayana Buddhism, one of the two major forms of Buddhism, became well known in China and offered salvation to its followers through the intercession of bodhisattvas, which are godlike beings.

Bushido—A code of ethics for the Japanese samurai, the warriors of the Japanese military aristocracy, requiring a life of austerity and self-discipline. This code of ethics was influenced by Confucian philosophy.

chun tzu—Literally, a gentleman. In Confucianism, a man of character who practices certain virtues. *see* FIVE VIRTUES

Confucian ethic—Confucian values, especially strong family structure, hard work, and love of learning.

Daoism—One of the three great faiths of China, emphasizing harmony with nature and an intuitive, rather than a rational, approach to life.

examination system—A system that tested one's knowledge of Confucian thought and allowed the selection of the academically talented to serve as mandarins, or scholar-officials. In order to pass these examinations candidates had to memorize the Confucian Five Classics and other works of Chinese literature.

filial piety—Respect and obedience toward one's parents. These obligations include the offering of sacrifices to the memory of one's parents after their death.

Five Classics—The most respected Confucian texts—those that Confucius referred to in his teaching: the *Book of Poetry*, the *Book of History*, the *Book of Rites*, the *Book of Changes*, and the *Spring and Autumn Annals*.

five elements—In Chinese science, the basic materials of all things: wood, metal, fire, water, and earth.

five relationships—As described by Confucius, the relationships in a well-ordered society: father/son, husband/wife, older brother/younger brother, friend/friend, ruler/subject.

five virtues—As described by Confucius, the traits of a Confucian gentleman who practices certain virtues. *see* LI, REN, XIN, YI, ZHI

Four Books—The four works that Neo-Confucianists added to the Five Classics: the *Analects*, the *Mencius*, the *Great Learning*, and the *Doctrine of the Mean*.

heaven—"*Tien*"; a spiritual force that influences human affairs, similar to the Western concept of providence.

jing—The Chinese word for "classic" and for "warp," the lengthwise threads of a woven fabric. Also a work of a particular time and place, whose truths are universal and timeless. Thus, to the Chinese, the Five Classics are the "warp" of their civilization.

Laozi—The founder of Daoism.

legalists—Followers of a school of Chinese thought that taught that the well-being of the state came before the individual, the antithesis of Confucius's view.

li—Correct behavior, the primary virtue in Confucius's philosophy. A word meaning "principle," the basic element in the Neo-Confucian philosophy of Zhu Xi.

mandarin—A scholar-official who had passed the imperial exams and who served as an official of the empire.

Mandate of Heaven—A Chinese emperor's right to rule.

Mencius—Mengzi, the greatest figure in Confucianism after Confucius himself, whose teachings are collected in the *Mencius*. Mencius believed that all people were born good and that each person should strive to find his or her inner self through study.

Neo-Confucianism—A form of Confucianism developed during the Song dynasty (960–1279), combining elements of Buddhism and Daoism with traditional Confucianism.

ren—Benevolence or humanity; one of the five virtues in Confucius's philosophy.

Sacred Edict of 16 Articles—A proclamation issued by the Kangxi emperor in 1672, consisting of maxims summarizing Confucian principles in simple language. Until the 20th century it was regularly read aloud in each Chinese school and village.

state Confucianism—The official form of Confucianism adopted by the rulers of the Han dynasty (202 B.C.E.–220 C.E.), incorporating some aspects of legalism and other ideas on the nature of the universe.

three faiths—Confucianism, Daoism, and Buddhism.

xin—Faithfulness or integrity; one of the five virtues in Confucius's philosophy.

yi—Honesty or uprightness; one of the five virtues in Confucius's philosophy.

yin and yang—The two countervailing forces of the universe, each necessary for balance yet each constantly changing in power.

zhi—Knowledge in the sense of moral wisdom; one of the five virtues in Confucius's philosophy.

INDEX

ABOUT THE AUTHOR

Dorothy and **Thomas Hoobler** have written more than 80 books for young readers, including several award-winning works on Asian history and culture. They live in New York City.

ABOUT THE SERIES EDITORS

Martin Palmer is the founder of ICOREC (International Consultancy on Religion, Education, and Culture) in 1983 and is the secretary-general of the Alliance of Religions and Conservation (ARC). He is the author of many books on world religions.

Joanne O'Brien has an M.A. degree in theology and has written a range of educational and general reference books on religion and contemporary culture. She is co-author, with Martin Palmer and Elizabeth Breuilly, of *Religions of the World* and *Festivals of the World* published by Facts On File Inc.

PICTURE CREDITS